Are You Puzzled By The Puzzle Of Life?

Lessons To Remember As You Pursue Your Purpose

Paul Vitale

with Heather Ericson

ISBN: 978-0-9666174-0-5

Fourth Printing

Printing
Walsworth Publishing Company

Design and Art Direction
Chuck Robertson

Photography
Drew Harris

Internal Editors
Twanette Goodnight and Debra Robinson

Graphics
Patrick Burnett

Print Production
Greg Shira

Before We Begin

There are many with whom we come in contact during our time on this earth. Some touch the deepest parts of our minds and souls, while others only scratch the surface. I dedicate this book to the three individuals who have found their way into my mind and soul and left an everlasting impression. To my mother, father and brother for always listening, but most importantly, for believing. Thank you for teaching me how to live for today and plan for tomorrow.

"I expect to pass through this world but once.
Any good thing, therefore, that I can do…
let me do it now… for I shall
not pass this way again."

– Attributed to Stephen Grellet

A Special Thanks

I would like to take a moment to shine the spotlight on those who inspired me and guided me through the writing process of this book. To Heather, my true friend, thank you for your thoughts, ideas and honest criticisms. There is no way I could have finished this project without you. To all of my friends and family at Cranford Johnson Robinson Woods advertising agency in Little Rock, Arkansas, I'll never be able to thank you enough for all the things you've taught me. To all of the people who were gracious enough to take the time to share their thoughts and perspectives, and last but not least, to you, the reader, for trusting the lessons and concepts within this book enough to take the time to pick it up and journey with me.

Lessons To Remember
As You Pursue Your Purpose

Why This Book of Lessons...

It is not unusual for me to do things backwards. For example, there are times when I will read a magazine from the last page to the first or attempt the piecing together of a puzzle without first looking at the picture on the front of the box. That's why I wasn't surprised when I found myself writing the introduction of this book after completing the last chapter.

After reading the finished manuscript, I knew that the best way to begin this journey was to let you know not only why I wrote this book, but also what knowledge I personally gained from it.

The idea to write a book originated from a conversation with my older brother. He asked, "Paul, in your opinion, what does it take to be successful?"

I pondered the question and decided that I didn't know, but was bound and determined to find out. Though I wasn't sure how to go about this task, I started by asking people who I thought were successful what it took for them.

I was so impressed with the answers I received that I decided to compile them so I could share them with others. When I started putting the responses together, I was able to group them into "lessons." I felt like they contained excellent information we could all benefit from during our journey of finding a purpose.

Every person I asked suggested a different route to finding success, varying from a strong work ethic to a good attitude to setting goals for yourself and working at all costs to achieve them.

Even though the answers were different, they all shared a common theme – a theme that defined success as finding your purpose and doing something that you love.

Only then did I understand that the answers weren't paths to take in order to find "success." They were things to do and qualities to have in order to find your passion and purpose – through this, you find happiness and success finds you.

–Paul Vitale

1

You Can't Finish
Unless You Begin

When I was ten years old, I had a life-changing experience that introduced me to the wonderful feeling of importance – if only for one shining moment. The event occurred at Three Rivers Stadium in Pittsburgh, Pennsylvania, the night I attended my first professional baseball game.

I was sitting in the stands with my popcorn and coke in hand watching the Pittsburgh Pirates play the San Diego Padres. I was having the time of my life when one of the Padres stepped up to the plate and hit a foul ball. Although this may not sound like such an unusual occurrence, for me this ball was a catalyst that started a chain of events which made that night go down in my history.

I stood up and was looking for the ball when I suddenly noticed a white blur headed my way. Before I had a chance to move, the ball struck me with a strong blow to the chest.

The next thing I knew, my father was at my side asking if I was okay. I tried to speak but could not because the breath had been knocked out of me. The stadium's medical crew came and rushed me downstairs to the emergency room where they x-rayed my chest. The doctor informed me that I had three bruised ribs, but once he taped me up, I would be fine to finish watching the game.

At that point, I was ready to go home. Overriding my opinion, my father insisted that we go back and finish the game. For obvious reasons, I wasn't exactly thrilled at the prospect of returning to the stands – then everything changed.

As we headed back to take our seats, a man looked at me and said, "Aren't you the little boy who got hit with the foul ball?" I nodded my head and he stood, shook my hand, then gave me the infamous baseball. Then another stood and shook my hand. Suddenly, one by one, people were standing and shaking my hand. Then the game stopped. Before I knew it, the entire crowd was on their feet giving me a standing ovation. As if the ovation weren't amazing enough, I looked up and saw myself on the big screen.

At that moment, I truly knew what it was like to feel special. Thousands of total strangers cared enough about my well-being that they stopped the game just to let me know that they were glad I was okay. To this day, I can still distinctly remember the feeling I had that night.

A stadium of people, who I will never have the opportunity to thank, unknowingly helped me pinpoint what it is I want to do with my life.

Reflecting on this one event, I realized that one of my purposes in life was to try to make everyone with whom I came in contact understand that, even if they weren't getting a standing ovation at Three Rivers Stadium, they were certainly special enough to deserve one.

Gathering the Pieces

Life is a gift, even though sometimes it's difficult to treat it as one. We live in a cruel, unjust world, where many lose the chance to live at a young age, while others waste their lives away. Searching for a purpose and a niche can drive you if you allow it to. If you approach life as an awesome opportunity to make an everlasting mark, you can.

I'm sure you have heard someone say, "Life is like a game." In some respects, this is true, but in my opinion, life is more like a puzzle. Pieces surround us, and we have to figure out how to position them in a way that makes sense.

Anyone who has ever sat down to put a puzzle together knows that before you can start matching pieces, you generally have to go through every single piece to find the edge pieces. After that, you have to go through them all again to find the pieces that have a certain color, and then again to find pieces that you missed the first couple of times. After grouping the pieces, the next step is determining where they fit. You have to constantly sort through all of the pieces until every piece is in its designated place and the puzzle is finished.

In my analogy, every person is an individual piece. It takes all kinds, colors, shapes and sizes to make the world complete. Like a puzzle, each person must be in his or her proper place.

This concept seems easy, but finding your distinct place can be overwhelming. Often you think a piece goes in a certain place, only to realize later that it wasn't an exact fit and that it fits much better someplace else.

You may have to try several different jobs before you find the one you can be passionate about and believe was meant for you or you may have to attend a variety of classes to determine your major. In any case, while you are searching, you are discovering many things that you are certain you don't want to do and learning new things about yourself.

Generally speaking, it takes a while to find your niche. Not only is it okay to keep searching, it's encouraged.

Search, Search And Keep Searching

Growing up, I always asked my father what the purpose of living was. He always answered this question with one word – Mankind! We live for X number of years building a strong reputation, financial success, a home, a family and then we die. We cannot take anything with us, so why do we try to obtain these things, let alone anything else?

If you can find a way to help better mankind while you're on this earth, you have done your job. People depend on other people each day to help them find what they are searching for and to make them feel as though their existence matters. If you can do this, then your time on earth has been well spent.

Understand that at times, no matter how much searching we do, the answers will not automatically appear. Generally we have the opportunity to make our own decisions, but other times circumstances beyond our control bring on change and transitions which make our decisions for us. Transitions will often lead us down paths which we may not have taken if we had a choice, yet once we are down that path, we see that we like where we are headed. Sometimes these external forces will lead us to change direction and see things from a different perspective. It's vital that in these times of change, you never quit searching for your purpose, because it will often appear in the most unexpected places.

We have all spent countless hours asking ourselves why our existence matters. Why were we given the miracle of life and what are we supposed to do with it? Constant questioning such as this brings constant learning. Never quit questioning and always try to recognize the answers when they come.

Follow Your Passion

Searching for your purpose can be frustrating, but the feeling when it is finally unveiled to you is one of the most amazing feelings you will ever have.

Amelia Earhart's story is an excellent example of discovering your purpose and following your passion. After World War I, many daredevil pilots from the war began having airshows to demonstrate the astonishing feats they could perform. Ms. Earhart attended one of these shows and three days later took her first plane ride. In her book *The Fun of It* (1932) she wrote, "I knew myself I had to fly.... 'I think I'd like to fly,' I told my family casually that evening, knowing full well I'd die if I didn't." She had seen what she was born to do and nothing could stop her.

Many have had the great fortune of understanding that feeling. Once your passion and purpose in life have been revealed to you, there is no barricade so large that it could deter you from going full force. Look forward to being passionate toward the things that matter to you. Grab them and hold on, for it's passion that makes your purpose come to life.

Take the Leap of Faith

I have discovered that you have to do whatever it takes to follow your passion and find your purpose. You may have to take a risk, leave a job or move to a new town. In any case, you have to take a leap of faith. Ronald E. McNair, an American astronaut who died in the *Challenger* space shuttle explosion, gave great advice when he said, "You can only become a winner if you are willing to walk over the edge."

Try to quit worrying about the little things and the possible outcomes. Stressing about small things over which you have no control only clutters your thoughts and wastes valuable time.

You really bring yourself down with many pointless worries and questions.

When I find myself trying to control the outcome, I reflect on the often quoted Serenity Prayer: *God, grant me the serenity to accept the things I cannot change, courage to change the things I can and the wisdom to know the difference.* We are here for such a short time. Keep life as simple as possible.

Writing this book has been somewhat risky for me – I am sharing my thoughts, ideas and opinions freely, which opens me up for criticism. At the same time, if it helps even one person, then without hesitation, it was certainly worth the risk. If I can have a direct or indirect hand in helping those around me, then I have done something that does matter. It all starts by taking a leap.

Simply Said...

You can't finish unless you begin.

- First, you have to "gather your pieces." Every person is an individual piece, and it takes all kinds, colors, shapes and sizes to make the world complete.
- Second, you have to keep searching. Constant questioning brings constant learning.
- Third, you have to follow your passion. Passion makes your purpose come to life.
- Fourth, take a leap of faith. You may have to take a risk, leave a job or move to a new town. In any case, you have to take that leap.

Remember that every ending has a beginning and the only way to start is to start.

Wise Words From Others...

I have brought myself, by long meditation, to the conviction that a human being with a settled purpose must accomplish it, and that nothing can resist a will which will stake even existence upon its fulfillment.

– Benjamin Disraeli

No man can be ideally successful until he has found his place. Like a locomotive he is strong on the track, but weak anywhere else.

– Orison Swett Marden

There is some place where your specialness can shine. Somewhere that difference can be expressed. It's up to you to find it, and you can.

– David Viscott

There is one quality, which one must possess to win, and that is definiteness of purpose, the knowledge of what one wants, and a burning desire to possess it.

– Napoleon Hill

If you don't know where you are going, how can you expect to get there?

– Basil S. Walsh

Visualize this thing that you want. See it, feel it, believe in it. Make your mental blueprint, and begin to build!

– Robert Collier

That's why many fail – because they don't get started – they don't go. They don't overcome inertia. They don't begin.

– W. Clement Stone

Everyone who got where he is had to begin where he was.

– Richard L. Evans

Set goals and objectives for tomorrow and the days following. Prepare yourself for where you want to be, not for where you are. Don't measure yourself by what you have accomplished, but by what you should have accomplished with your ability.

– Henry Nichols, President of
Central and Southern Companies, Inc.

One has to act on what they know. You already have within you what you need to succeed. Take action, and if one action doesn't work, change your approach. As Thomas Edison said, "I am not discouraged, because every wrong attempt discarded is another step forward."

– Anthony Robbins, Chairman of the Board
Robbins Research International, Inc.

2
Achieve The Ultimate Balance

Finding a balance in this fast-paced world can be a never-ending quest. Many have the great fortune of finding a true balance between the things they cherish in their hearts and the "must do's" of life. Others never have this satisfaction.

I have recognized that a happy person is able to find a common thread and weave it through the most meaningful aspects of his or her life. This can be financial success, a love for others, family or achievements in the workplace. You have to decide for yourself what aspects really make your blood flow, your mind race and your heart open.

If you are like me, trying to find a balance will keep you up at night and will stay on your mind throughout the day. Three aspects of my life that keep me on my toes and that I continually attempt to balance are my spiritual life, professional life and personal life. How can I focus daily on any one of these, let alone all of them?

Although achieving balance is never easy, the times when it is needed most are times of transition. These times can include graduating from high school or college, moving or changing jobs. Take a moment to think back to the last time you went through a transitional stage in your life and try to recall how you attained a level of balance.

Graduating from college was my last major transition. When I graduated and left the comfort zone of college, my life completely changed. I achieved the goal of graduating and had to move on to the next goal, which was a little more tricky – I had to find a job, a place to live, a church, friends, etc. In college, many things are in place for you – you have a roommate, a place to sleep, a place to eat, a routine and so on. Once you enter the "working world," you are on your own to find many of these things.

This was a point in my life where I knew I needed to find a new focal point – something that would keep me on the right road toward the type of person I wanted to become. I learned that there were several qualities I needed if I wanted a balanced life.

Sharpen Your Focus

Begin by sharpening your focus.

Focus will help give you direction, and you must have direction before you can begin working toward your goals. Anyone who has ever set a goal and focused on it 100% will tell you that it completely empowers you to achieve. Alex Trotman, the Chairman of the Board of Ford Motor Company, relayed it very simply. He said, "One has to have many great qualities, such as integrity, determination and flexibility, but without setting goals, one is not as likely to succeed." Mr. Trotman has a good point. You have to be able to place your energy and brainpower toward one or two things and focus on them in order to be successful.

Many times we have to step away from a project or task so we can refocus. Often things don't go our way, and we have to change our approach. Don't be afraid to do this anytime it's necessary.

If you are focused on making an "A" on an exam, and you are studying your materials with the help of flash cards, but are not getting the information down, then change your approach. Ask another student to help explain what you don't comprehend. Use various study aids, but do something different so you can begin understanding. Rarely is there only one road to lead you to your destination. If you hit a dead end, turn around and try another road.

For example, one of my goals has always been to be a public speaker. I want to be able to touch the lives of others and help them succeed. I have had to travel many different avenues in order to reach this goal. Writing letters to other speakers asking for their advice, studying video and audio tapes for pointers and having others critique my seminars are just a few roads I have had to travel. Though I have not reached my goal in its entirety, I believe I am taking the proper steps in learning all I can about the goal on which I am focused.

To focus and refocus is challenging. Don't be intimidated by this idea. Accept this fact and allow faith to lead you.

Let Faith Lead You

Having a focus is a good start, but where do you go from there? How do you take your focus and turn it into reality? For me, this is where faith has always stepped in. You first have to obtain the knowledge and skills necessary to achieve the goal on which you are focused. Then you must have faith in God, yourself and those around you to know that you can accomplish that goal. Believe in yourself and don't let failure intimidate you.

People fear failure. No one wants to be embarrassed in front of others, so many never get up and state how they feel. No one wants to lose a business account or project, so many do not bid on it in the first place. No one wants to be rejected by a potential mate, so many never take a chance to initiate a relationship.

During times like these, we have to understand that failure will happen, but we must have the faith to know that if we keep trying, eventually we will succeed.

Faith comes in many different forms. If you believe that one form works better for you than another, then you should believe that wholeheartedly and not let others sway your opinion.

Have you ever noticed how superstitious athletes are? For instance, some basketball players will place their sock on their right foot before their left, or they will wear a certain piece of clothing during every game hoping that it will bring good luck. One example is Michael Jordan. He wears a pair of North Carolina shorts under his Chicago Bulls shorts every game because he says it makes him feel comfortable so that he can perform to his fullest potential.

This sounds absurd, but the next time you go to a professional baseball game, count how many players step on the chalk lines. You will be surprised to see how many do not. Many baseball players believe that if they step on the chalk line, it will bring them bad luck.

These superstitions are forms of faith for these athletes. No one could convince them that this type of faith is in any way inferior to another form. In their minds, their focus on winning is directly affected by this faith.

Although it is important to have faith that you will succeed in your endeavors, another extremely important faith is faith in the unknown. We have to be able to take what life gives us and trust that we will not be given more than we can handle and that eventually things will work out.

I experienced faith in action on a plane trip home from Raleigh, North Carolina. Although I was originally supposed to sit in one seat, I was moved to another upon boarding. Changing seats gave me the opportunity to visit with one of the nicest and most sincere people I have ever met.

In the seat next to mine was a woman who had three sons living in various parts of the country. She was returning home after spending the holiday season with one of her sons and his family in Raleigh. She had raised her children to be productive members of society, she had beautiful grandchildren, she was financially secure and able to spend time with her loved ones. It would seem life was treating this woman well. Yet, after speaking with her, I learned that the son she had visited in Raleigh had a brain tumor and only a 25% chance of surviving. She explained to me how the doctors found the tumor and what procedures had been performed to attempt to rid her son of this deadly disease.

From that point on, this became one of the most emotional plane trips I had ever taken. I asked her how she coped with the pain and the sense of the unknown. She said that faith was the only thing she knew would never leave her, so she hung on to it and took everything else in stride. This was coming from a woman who lost her husband ten years before and was faced with soon losing her son.

I was moved by the strength of this seventy-seven-year-old woman. You could see the courage in her eyes, and it was easy to see that faith helped place it there. She was prepared to make the most out of even the worst of what life could bring.

It doesn't matter what form of faith you choose to believe in, as long as you are disciplined enough to believe in it fully each day of your life.

Develop Discipline

To achieve balance, you must have discipline.

Decide what is truly worthwhile to you and what is not. Discipline yourself enough to take the time to determine your top priorities.

If your family is one of the most valuable aspects of your life, then be disciplined enough to put other things aside and spend quality time with them. Give them the attention and love that they deserve. Even though we often place our family on the back burner, we must take advantage of every opportunity we have to spend time with them. They depend on it and are worth it.

If you are striving to have a successful career, then you must realize on the front end that work takes time. My uncle once told me, "Paul, you can't be afraid to work. If you are going to make your mark in life, you have to work for it."

I come from the type of family that believes in doing your part. My mother always taught me the importance of a strong work ethic through simple chores around the house. I knew that each day I had to empty the dishwasher, take out the trash and clean my room. There were no excuses for not getting this done. Through this, I learned discipline and a strong work ethic. If I didn't do my chores or did them poorly, there would be consequences for my actions.

Whether or not the word discipline is a part of your vocabulary is up to you. It doesn't matter where you are or what you are striving for, becoming a disciplined person will help you enormously in reaching your goals. Although the concept sounds easy, it takes a lot of work and can be extremely challenging. If you want something in life, and are disciplined enough to work to obtain it, then the results will be well worth the effort.

Living Dedicated

To be dedicated to a project, to a loved one or to anything else in life means doing whatever it takes to get the job done.

There are many who are born with natural talents. They have the ability to accomplish tasks without a lot of work or preparation. We all know people like this. There are also many who may not have been blessed with innate abilities, yet they can still reach their goals – they just have to work a little harder. This is where dedication comes into play.

Allow dedication to take over, help you improve certain areas and give you a reason to never give up. Patti Upton, the founder of Aromatique Inc., a world leader in the development of home fragrances, said, "You must have ability, dedication and work ethic to succeed."

Be committed enough to finish what you start. If you say that you are going to complete a project, then be totally devoted to it. Let your will shine through during the times that you feel like you are up against the world. There will always be someone else more qualified, better educated or better known, but will they be more dedicated than you? The answer to this question is totally up to you.

Athletes of all ages must be dedicated. They have to first define their task, whether it is to get stronger, bigger or faster. Then they must have the discipline to reach their tasks. How did Cal Ripkin Jr. play 2,131 baseball games and break Lou Gehrig's record? When Rocky Bleier came back from Vietnam with shrapnel injuries and was told that he would never play football again, how did he go on to play running back for the four-time Super Bowl Champion Pittsburgh Steelers? How did Payton Manning stand up to all the pressure and make the decision to stay at Tennessee for his senior year to lead the Volunteers to a

SEC Football Championship? All of these questions can be answered with one word – dedication!

While watching the 1998 Winter Olympics, I was amazed at some of the stories about how the athletes train. Several of the athletes profiled knew when they were small children that they wanted to be the best in the world and were willing to give up a lot of things to achieve their goals. Many began as young as five years old, which took as much dedication from the parents as the child. They came home from school, and while other children were out playing with friends, they were training. This is dedication. They decided that they wanted something and then put everything they had into attaining it. When you choose something that you want, give it your best or live with wondering what might have been.

Dedication is key, not just for an athlete, but for everyone. If you are a student, you have to be dedicated enough to attend class, study and do your best to make the grades. No one will do this for you, so you have the ultimate choice to pass or fail. In any job field, you must be dedicated enough to make it to work on time, get your assignment and follow through. This will reflect on you and help you become better at what you do.

Don't place yourself on an unrealistic time schedule. Take your time to do things right for the right reasons, and you will find your own balance.

Simply Said...

You can achieve the ultimate balance.

- First, sharpen your focus. Focusing on a goal completely, empowers you to achieve.
- Second, let faith lead you. You have to believe in God, yourself and those around you enough to know that you can accomplish anything you desire.
- Third, develop discipline. If you want something in life and are disciplined enough to work to obtain it, then the results will be well worth the effort.

- Fourth, live dedicated. Do whatever it takes to get the job done.

Once you have achieved the victory of a balanced life, you will find that you have time for the things that you cherish, plus you will realize that the "must do's" of life aren't so bad.

Wise Words From Others...

Whether you think you can or think you can't – you're right.

– Henry Ford

Faith is not belief without proof, but trust without reservations.

– Elton Trueblood

Some things have to be believed to be seen.

– Ralph Hodgson

It is only with the heart that one can see rightly; what is essential is invisible to the eye.

– Antoine de Saint-Exupéry

Faith is different from proof; the latter is human, the former is a gift from God.

– Blaise Pascal

Success seems to be largely a matter of hanging on after others have let go.

– William Feather

Nothing in the world can take the place of persistence. Talent will not; nothing is more common than unsuccessful men with talent. Genius will not; unrewarded genius is almost a proverb. Education will not; the world is full of educated derelicts. Persistence and determination alone are omnipotent.

– Calvin Coolidge

To be a success, you must be a self-starter. You must be able to make yourself go to your office every morning, turn on the computer and begin, even when you have no idea what you're beginning. Then you must come up for air when the rest of your family needs or wants your presence.

– Patricia Lorenz, Writer

Success can be defined in so many different ways it is first important to determine what is most important to you – a close relationship, a family, a home, a job, helping others or feeling valued by others. Then set out a place to achieve small successes, which will eventually lead to feelings of success.

> – Robert Reasoner, President
> International Council for Self-Esteem

Know yourself, your values, your strengths and weaknesses.

> – William Cavanaugh III, President & CEO
> Carolina Power & Light Company

3

The Power to Choose

Life is made up of many choices – choices that dictate how we live daily.

We are faced with choices from the minute we wake up to the minute we go to bed. What should I wear today? Should I take my lunch or go out? Should I buy a gift or just send a card? The list of everyday choices goes on and on.

When I was a high school senior, I had to make one of the toughest choices a young person has to make – which college to attend after graduation. Should I stay at the local university, live at home with my parents rent-free and play baseball on a scholarship or should I go to a university forty-five minutes away without all the extra perks? This was the point in my life when I was introduced to the school of choices.

Who knows what is right or wrong? And, in this particular case, who can say there was a right or wrong answer? Both public universities had strong academics, good athletic programs and the same entrance qualifications. It just made sense that I attend the local university. My parents wanted me to stay at home, where I had everything I needed – complete with a security blanket draped over me.

After much consideration, I decided which path I wanted to take toward my future. I chose to take the path that was not as comfortable and attend the university away from home.

Looking back on it today, I am glad I made that particular decision.

Now I can see how going away to college helped me grow tremendously. Because I chose to step out of my comfort zone, I learned many new things about life and myself – how to cook a few things (like grilled cheese, Tony's pizzas and pot pies); how to wash and iron (which thrilled my mother); and how to manage my finances (what little I had). I was on my own to make new friends, discipline myself to make it to class on time and understand that I was responsible for my actions.

If I had stayed at home, although I'm sure I would have learned a thing or two, I would have never learned many of the things a responsible adult needs to know. I was on my own, and I had to be accountable for my actions and for building a new foundation in a new place.

Making choices of this caliber will only help you make other decisions later in life. I once asked Anthony Robbins, the well-known motivational speaker, what his thoughts were on making decisions. He wrote back and said, "Paul, you have to practice making decisions and choices. You have to exercise your decision-making muscle just like you exercise your body. Once you learn to make small choices in life, the larger ones will be that much easier." I agree totally with Mr. Robbins' philosophy.

Practice making decisions and be thankful that you have the ability. The next time you become discouraged by the thought of all of the tough decisions you have to make, look around. Take note of the decisions others are making. Many will be equal to or even more difficult than yours.

Be totally honest with yourself first and then honest with those around you, and your decisions will come that much easier.

"Just Because" Doesn't Get It

How many times have you heard someone say that he or she chose to do something "just because"? I got this new hairstyle just because my best friend has one. I joined this particular group just because it's the thing to do. No matter what the reason, we must understand the reality of circumstances.

For every "just because," there is a set of circumstances that follows. I am leaving my job *just because* I do not get paid enough and my boss is the worst person to work for. I am leaving my wife and kids *just because* I am tired of being responsible for a family. I am going to experiment with pot *just because* everyone will call me a wimp if I don't. I am going to ask my girlfriend to marry me *just because* all of our friends are getting married. You can see that "just because" keeps showing up. Every one of these examples represents reality for many.

My father has always told me that life is about trading one set of circumstances for another. Before you make a "just because" decision, it is best to take the time to think about the new set of circumstances and consequences that will be headed your way.

If you quit that under-paying job before securing a new one, you may be faced with not getting paid at all. If you leave the family that you have created, you will be faced with the family of loneliness. If you begin smoking pot with your friends, you are faced with higher odds of hurting yourself or someone else. If you decide to get married just because everyone else is, there is a good chance that you will not be happy and that your marriage will not last. With each choice comes responsibility.

Take Responsibility For Your Choices

When you and I make our choices, we must keep in mind that we are totally responsible for them. Even though we don't often consider the consequences, they will always be there. Every day we are faced with choices that question our values, morals and ethics – choices that will either make us a better person for our decision or make us lose a lot of sleep. For example, have you ever been undercharged for a meal at a restaurant or walked out of a store and realized that you didn't pay? What did you do?

Did you return to correct the mistake or did you just walk away?

In situations like these, it's easy to tell yourself that it was an honest mistake and that it wasn't really your fault. Just because you didn't intentionally do anything wrong doesn't make it right. You are the only person who can make the decision to do the right thing. Others can tell you what they would do, but you are the one who has to crawl into bed at night and sleep with your choices.

Knowing this has really helped me understand that I have to make decisions for myself. Of course, I will listen to the opinions of those closest to me, but I know that the ultimate choice is mine and that I have to be responsible for the result.

Compare Your Options

Since decision-making has never really come easy for me, I have made it a habit to take time to analyze all my options and plan the next move. I take a piece of paper and write down the pros and cons so that I have something in front of me to study and review. This not only enables me to make a decision, it often gives me a new perspective. Plus, sometimes when I write things down, I see that the problem is not as insurmountable as I originally thought. This is a simple activity that can help anyone make his or her next move.

We all must realize that there are options for every decision with which we are faced. If you don't like what you are doing, then do something about it. So many, including myself, continue to do the same things because we are frightened by change. You return daily to the same job because you are too scared to look for something more challenging. You continue in the same relationship because you don't want to hurt the person you are with. You never begin a workout program because you are intimidated by what others at the gym might think.

Although these scenarios may sound familiar, they are excuses for not realizing your options. You have the option of whether or not to stay in that job, to continue in that relationship or to go to the gym. It is amazing how good it feels when you are doing the things that you want to be doing and that you truly believe in.

Take a minute to write down all of the things that you enjoy doing and all that you don't. You will be surprised at the things you see. If you see a lot of things you don't enjoy, then determine what your other options are and start making changes. I understand change is difficult. It's easy to get settled into a routine, but the reality is, if you aren't happy but won't change things, then who will?

Position Yourself

"We fail to see that we can control our own destiny; make ourselves do whatever is possible; make ourselves become whatever we long to be."

There is a lot of truth in this statement from Orison Swett Marden. We often set goals for ourselves, only to later see them go by the wayside, gone and forgotten. Any goal you set is attainable, but requires planning, perseverance and patience.

To plan for a goal is to map out exactly how you are going to go about achieving it. Positioning yourself properly is one of the best ways possible to see your vision through. Here are three examples of ways you can position yourself and create new opportunities.

If you want to start a lawn business in the summer to help pay for college, how do you begin? You begin by getting your name out.

One way to do this is to send out information about your business during the winter months. Explain your service to the potential customer and ask if you could have his or her business.

Then in the spring, follow-up with a personal visit to introduce yourself. Even if people don't need your service at that time, they probably will at some point. More than likely, they will recall the person who took such a strong initiative.

This is one simple example of positioning yourself.

Another way is through internship programs. I received my start in marketing and advertising through this avenue. A year before I graduated from college, I began searching for potential internships. I found one that I thought I would like and before I knew it, I was given an opportunity to intern. After the program was complete, I was offered a full-time job with the company. Thus, I not only found an internship, I put myself in a position to be offered a job.

Volunteering is another wonderful way to position yourself. Many organizations, groups, offices and medical facilities are always searching for volunteers. Through giving of your time generously, you will not only be helping others, you will be helping yourself. Networking with others and demonstrating your ability to work will help you tremendously. When an organization needs someone they can depend on to get the job done, they will likely think of you.

You must take the initiative to reach your fullest potential. It does take time and patience, but if you persevere, the rewards will be worth it.

Develop A Strong Work Ethic

All the positioning in the world will not do any good unless you have equipped yourself with a strong work ethic. We all have the opportunity to strive 100% toward the goals we set. If we allow it, work ethic will be the automobile that helps us accomplish those goals.

I would be lying if I said that being successful does not take hard work. It does! You and I have to be willing to go the extra mile and keep our heads up while we're doing it.

I have heard many say, "I don't have a strong work ethic because no one taught me how to work." I don't buy this. When you wanted to set up your first lemonade stand as a child, you had to work to make it happen. You had to create a stand, find the lemonade mix, make it, and go out and sell it. This took work. You wanted to accomplish something, and you did. When you wanted to work for an allowance from your parents so you could buy a bicycle or you wanted to get your first job so you could work toward your first car, you had to be willing to use your work ethic. If you want something badly enough, you will do whatever it takes to get it.

Develop a strong work ethic by being prompt, being detailed, and doing things right the first time. You will still make mistakes, but not as many as you would without a strong work ethic.

Simply Said...

You have the power to choose.

- First, remember that "just because" doesn't get it. Before you make a "just because" decision, think about the new set of circumstances and consequences that will follow.
- Second, compare your options. Write down all of the pros and cons so you can have a clear picture of where you are and where you want to be.
- Third, position yourself. Make yourself known through internships, volunteering and serving others.
- Fourth, develop a strong work ethic. You choose whether or not to give 100% of yourself to the tasks before you.

Remember that everything you do is something you have chosen to do. Make choices wisely and always remember that with each choice comes not only responsibility, but also opportunity.

Wise Words From Others...

You are where you are today because you have chosen to be there.

– Harry Browne

We fail to see that we can control our own destiny; make ourselves do whatever is possible; make ourselves become whatever we long to be.

– Orison Swett Marden

You always do what you want to do. This is true with every act. You may say that you had to do something or that you were forced to, but actually, whatever you do, you do by choice. Only you have the power to choose for yourself.

– W. Clement Stone

The key to your universe is that you can choose.

– J. Martin Kohe

When you take charge of your life, there is no longer need to ask permission of other people or society at large.... When you ask permission, you give someone veto power over your life.

– Geoffry F. Abert

Sometimes if you want to see a change for the better, you have to take things into your own hands.

– Clint Eastwood

We forfeit three-fourths of ourselves in order to be like other people.

– Arthur Schopenhauer

4

Relationships:
The Support System of Life

No one person makes it through this world alone.

It doesn't matter whether it's a mother and daughter, a father and son or a worker and co-worker, we all depend on relationships. Some relationships blossom and grow, while others never get off the ground. In any case, we are taught valuable lessons that cannot be learned in a classroom or from a book.

It is vital that we have those who can help guide us down certain roads, stop us from going down others and walk beside us as we travel roads unknown. These relationships will often be the saving grace that we need when times are tough and will give us a greater appreciation for the good times.

From family to friends to business associates – embrace each relationship with an open mind and a willingness to give more than you receive. For the foundation begins with you and is built upon by others.

The Family Foundation

The first relationship we encounter is with our family. These are the people who teach us to love unconditionally, care about others, play fair and share. Usually, this relationship is one that will last a lifetime.

Families give us our memories, teach us our values and love us in a way that nobody else can. At the same time, they can also hurt and disappoint us. Through these lessons, our families help us build a foundation for all of our future relationships, both personal and professional. Take the time to recognize this and make an effort to learn from it.

Value Friendships

Generally speaking, everyone has friends before they are able to understand what friendship is. When you were young, you needed friends for playmates. It was always more fun to have someone around who was close to your age and enjoyed playing the same things.

As you grew older, you became more selective when choosing close friends. You probably have similar interests with many, but often there are some with whom you don't have much in common – yet for whatever reason, you just seem to click. We don't know why some people are put into our lives, but I am convinced that everyone who passes through was put there for a reason.

True friends are hard to find and even harder to replace. When you are fortunate enough to find a true friend, you have found a treasure. Treat your friends with honesty and respect. If you say you are going to do something or be somewhere, follow through. Your word is your bond. These individuals are ones you can depend on when you think the world is coming to an end. However, the converse is also true – they should be able to depend on you.

In friendships, as with all relationships, we must balance expectations with realities. If you reflect on past relationships, you can probably see that the times when you got hurt were when your expectations went unfulfilled. False hopes and unrealistic expectations are the downfall of many unsuccessful relationships.

I'm not suggesting that you try not to have any expectations, just that they be realistic. In my past relationships, I have learned that the only way to ensure that neither party has unrealistic expectations is to be completely honest 100% of the time.

Keep that in mind each day. Do not undervalue your friends, because one day they may not be there. We all have the opportunity to meet many people, but we should consider ourselves blessed if we have the opportunity to meet a true friend.

Relationships in Business

It's to your advantage to build solid relationships in any field of business. You have the opportunity each day to surround yourself with positive influences. These influences and relationships can help you if you allow them.

First, build strong alliances with your co-workers. It is always good to have someone within your office you can trust and vice-versa. In the business world, like in life, you never know when you may need someone on your side. American Industrial

Psychologist Stuart Margulies was quoted as saying, "People are rarely fired for incompetence. It's not getting along that's almost always the underlying reason for dismissal."

Learn to be loyal to your colleagues. When a conflict arises, go straight to the source. Discuss that problem with the person directly involved instead of talking negatively about him in his absence. When people talk about others negatively, it only makes the speaker come across as someone who is knocking others down to bring himself or herself up. Talking negatively will not solve your problem, it will only create more. Give your loyalty to others, and they will give you theirs in return.

In my grandfather's house, I came across a poem from the 1940s that hung in the offices of the Pittsburgh Water Heater Corporation. Although some of the language is different than what we would use today, the message still applies. It read:

If you want to work for the kind of a firm

Like the kind of a firm you like,

You needn't slip your clothes in a grip

Or start on a job-hunting hike.

You'll only find what you left behind,

For there's nothing that's really new.

It's a knock at yourself when you knock your boss.

It isn't the firm. It's you!

No company's made by men who are afraid

Lest somebody else gets ahead.

When everyone works and nobody shirks

You can bring back a business that's dead.

And if, while you make your personal stake,

Your fellows can make one, too,

Your firm will be what you want it to be.

It isn't the firm. It's you!

These principles are timeless. Work hard, be loyal to your company and your colleagues, and success will follow.

Second, understand the importance of networking. The more contacts you have, the more options you have. There's an old saying, "It's not what you know, but who." In most cases, this is true. Not to discount knowledge – that is always first and foremost – but knowing people certainly won't hurt you when you are trying to make a name for yourself.

Third, be careful not to burn too many bridges. Even if you are working with someone you don't particularly care for, give him or her your best effort. You never know when you may need that person's assistance down the road. It is amazing how small the world really is and chances are you will cross paths with these people later.

Fourth, surround yourself with the right people and the right teams. You have to be smart. You will often notice yourself becoming more and more like the people with whom you associate, so be careful to choose people who are positive influences and who will allow you to grow and mature in your profession.

You have the opportunity to make business relationships work for you. Remember – give more than you take, be loyal to your team and follow through on your word. Do this and people will not only know who you are – they will remember you.

Follow Through

Your follow through is crucial to accomplishing or achieving, yet more importantly, it is your word. If you have a client that you promised materials to by a certain date, then it is in your best interest to deliver. If you tell a friend you will meet him or her at a certain time, be there. Obviously, there will be times that you have outside barriers that interfere. Make sure that you call and explain why you can't do what you had agreed to. This will reflect your reliability and will show others that you genuinely care.

Following through on personal tasks or assignments is equally as important as following through for others. If you can't trust yourself to follow through, then you will have a difficult time believing that others will.

When I started writing this book, I must say that I had my own doubts about whether I would ever finish it. But once I got started, I knew that I had to finish, if only because I had said I would. The way I look at it, your word is all of the accountability you need. You have to be accountable to yourself first. Only then can you be accountable to others.

Give your total support and commitment to the activities to which you agree and allow others to see your progress. It is always a great idea to keep people in the loop. Taking the time to let them know how things stand makes them feel important – and remember they are!

When You Are Alone, Don't Be

There are many people who have to have someone around them all the time. The majority of people I have met seem to be the happiest when they are surrounded by others. This type of person blossoms when others notice them and listen to their ideas. This is how they grow and achieve self-fulfillment, which is why they are called "people-persons."

On the other hand, there are individuals who would much rather be paddling through this life alone. They would prefer to sit in a room by themselves rather than interact with other people. This is why these people are called "self-doers."

Throughout the past few years of my life, I have experienced a little of both personalities. I'm the type of person who has to have people around me most of the time. Of course, I enjoy the occasional quiet time just like the rest, but I have to have personal contact with others. I like hearing others' thoughts and ideas, as well as getting to express mine. The majority of the time, I would definitely characterize myself as a "people-person."

There are many times though that circumstances will force us to be alone. These are the times when "people-persons" have to become "self-doers."

I have had the opportunity to travel to different cities and states over the past few years. Those of you who travel know what it is like to stay in hotels night after night and to sit in different restaurants eating your meals alone. I have experienced loneliness during times that I should have been experiencing life.

Through this, I have learned that there is no better time to sit and reflect, write, read or dream than when you are eating a meal by yourself. When you are alone, do your best not to be.

When I know that I will be on my own for an extended period of time – whether at home or while traveling – I try to have many different materials on hand. When traveling, I always take a newspaper, magazine or book into the restaurant with me if I am dining alone. If I am not reading, then I am creating my "to do list" for the next day. I do my very best never to waste an hour. This works for me in my hotel room, as well – while there, I am either writing or working out. During these times, I also enjoy going to area attractions to educate myself about the history or culture of the city where I am staying.

Use your time wisely and get ahead of the game. Keep as busy as you can learning as much as you can. By doing this, you will also get to know yourself better and begin to view "alone time" as something other than negative.

This also applies to students in college. During my first semester at the university, I did not want to be around anyone. I was intimidated by what the people on campus would think of me.

I sat in my room night after night looking at the walls and wasting time.

My schedule was the same every day – go to class, eat in the cafeteria and go straight back to my room. Finally one night, I tried something brand new. I obtained a list of celebrity addresses from a baseball coach, took the list and began writing letters to various athletes, celebrities, musicians and spokespersons.

I started with the people that I most admired. I explained to them how much I looked up to them and then I asked if they would take a moment to send me an autographed photo. I must say that I never thought anything would come of this hobby.

After two weeks, I received my first autographed picture from the legendary country singer, George Strait. I immediately became hooked. I wrote several letters a week for three years. All of a sudden, I found something to do with the time I was wasting staring at the walls. I created a new hobby, while finding a new sense of confidence.

When I walked into the campus post office, people would ask me why I was receiving letters from movie stars, entertainers and other noteworthy people. You can only imagine some of the stories I told. Through that small idea, I was able to collect hundreds of autographs. This turned into a very lucrative way to pass the time while I was alone.

Do your best to make the best use of your time. There is so much to discover in this world if you only take advantage of every minute of every hour of every day.

To have successful relationships, we have to be comfortable with ourselves. If you are a "people-person," learn to sometimes be a "self-doer." If we learn to be honest with ourselves, we learn to be honest with others. If we can enjoy our own company, we can enjoy the company of others that much more.

Simply Said...

Relationships are the support system of life.

- First, start with the family foundation. Within the family, we first learn how to relate to other people.

- Second, value friendships. True friends are hard to find and even harder to replace. When you have found a true friend, you have found a treasure.

- Third, build good business relationships. It is vital to understand the importance of networking and to be careful not to burn bridges.

- Fourth, follow through. Your follow through is crucial not only to accomplishing or achieving, but more importantly, because it is your word.

- Fifth, when you are alone, don't be. Know the difference between solitude and loneliness, and learn to enjoy and make the best use of the times when you are alone.

Relationships can be complex, but they make the world go 'round. Do your best to get the most out of every one you have the opportunity to experience. Some of the best advice on this subject comes from Ralph Waldo Emerson, who said, "The only way to have a friend is to be one."

Wise Words From Others...

Personal relationships are the fertile soil from which all advancement, all success, all achievement in real life grows.

– Ben Stein

There is no such thing as a self-made man. You will reach your goals only with the help of others.

– George Shinn

No young man starting in life could have better capital than plenty of friends. They will strengthen his credit, support him in every great effort, and make him what, unaided, he could never be. Friends of the right sort will help him more – to be happy and successful – than much money....

– Orison Swett Marden

To fail to love is not to exist at all.

> – Mark Van Doren

If I have lost every other friend on earth, I shall at least have one friend left, and that friend shall be down inside of me.

> – Abraham Lincoln

My best friend is the one who brings out the best in me.

> – Henry Ford

The most important single ingredient in the formula of success is knowing how to get along with people.

> – Theodore Roosevelt

5

Perception Is Reality

The perception a person has of you in his or her mind is reality.

People draw conclusions very quickly. This is why it is beneficial to make a good first impression. Although you do not have total control of the perceptions others have of you, you do have the ability to influence their opinions through your actions, as well as the people with whom you associate.

Since your actions speak volumes, there are several ways you can make sure they say what you want in order to improve the likelihood that others will have the perception of you that you desire.

Maintain Composure

Have you ever stood in line at a grocery store when the person in front of you was not completely organized? Their check would not clear, they had no cash and an extra trip to the dairy section was necessary because they forgot the milk. It is easy to lose your patience at a time like this. With all of the distractions, responsibilities and worries, you have to find a way to stay composed.

Remaining composed is often one of the most effective ways to combat negative situations. For instance, normally things go smoothly when I am presenting a marketing and advertising plan. But there will always be that one time when the client just does not like the proposal. He or she thinks that the creative work is far from being creative, or they think we shouldn't place an ad in a certain publication even though the research says the return on investment would be great.

What do you do in a situation like this? Do you throw a fit and tell your client what you really think of him or her? Do you act or react? Although there are many times when you can't control external forces such as your client's opinion, you can always control your reaction.

If your reaction is composed and somewhat cool, you can think clearly and quickly on your feet. If you act on your instinct without thinking about what you plan to say, you might not ever have the opportunity to explain what you were trying to relay through your work. There is a good chance that spouting off without thinking will result in the loss of a client. Although it's difficult, you have to maintain your composure.

When people ask me how I do this, I usually tell them one thing – breathe!

You have to be able to take a deep breath and let all of the tension out so you can handle the negative situation. Breathing will automatically relax your muscles. After you take a deep breath, make sure you think about the situation before you begin speaking. If you speak before you think, more often than not, you will end up regretting what you said. After thinking about the best and most positive rebuttal, react to the situation. And remember that in most cases, it is better to say too little than too much.

Smart people study how others handle themselves during controversial times and learn from them. Take the time to watch how certain people handle key situations. Composed people will handle them with class and integrity, and will basically make the situation look easy. When watching others, notice that composure and patience go hand-in-hand.

It is much harder to remain composed when you lose your patience. I know that it is very difficult to be patient at times, but it can and will help you.

Have you ever been caught in bumper-to-bumper traffic at rush hour when you were already late for class or a meeting at the office? There is a car stalled in front of you, and you can't get around it. "Road rage" sets in and you basically want to pull your hair out. This is when patience comes into play. Developing patience takes time, but there aren't many other options. You have to take a deep breath and wait it out. Many times when I begin to get totally frustrated, I will sing a song or try to find humor in the situation. Generally, this calms me down and allows me to regain my composure.

Childcare workers, hospital chaplains, police officers, 911 operators and doctors – just to name a few – all have to develop a high level of composure in their day-to-day jobs. Not only do their careers depend on it, but the individuals they are serving depend on it as well. I cannot imagine being a police officer during a hostage situation. Think about the composure and patience a police officer has to have when a criminal has a gun in his or her face.

As long as you are trying to develop patience and composure, you are moving in the right direction. These qualities take time to master, but when you have them, you will find that they are very useful in everyday living.

Surround Yourself With Positive People

Have you noticed that parents are fairly intuitive when it comes to their children's friends? You can bring a friend home and for some reason your parents just don't like him or her. You don't really know why, but as you grow older, it is often easier to look back and see little things about those friends that you may not have seen earlier. Your parents may not have wanted you to hang around with them because they knew that the perception people have of you depends a lot on those with whom you surround yourself.

Simply put, if you want people to perceive you as a kind, honest, courteous, respectful and hardworking person, then associate with others who have those qualities.

It is also to your advantage to work with people whose qualities you admire. Working with people who do not have a strong work ethic or who are not honest in their dealings will cause others to see you as this type of person. Even if you aren't like this, surrounding yourself with these types of people will cause you to foster some resentment toward them and their behavior.

People Are Always Watching

It doesn't matter where you are, what you are doing or what you are wearing, people are always watching you.

If you are walking to class with your backpack strapped to your shoulders or walking into the office with your briefcase in hand, people are watching you. If you are in the mall, at the park, at the symphony or at the circus, people are watching you. When you realize this, you will understand the importance of how you carry yourself, how you handle various situations with composure and how you treat others.

Knowing this, I have done my best to use it to my advantage. I have always felt that it was my responsibility to be a role model for others. We need to try to set good examples not only because people are watching, but also because it is a way to have some sort of accountability for our actions.

Keep in mind, sometimes perceptions can be wrong. Often your actions will look suspect to an outsider, when actually you are doing nothing out of the ordinary. Don't frown on this idea. If you know why people are getting the wrong perception, you can learn a great deal from them, as well as how to alter your behavior so that others don't get the same opinion.

Parents often say, "I know you aren't doing anything wrong and you know you aren't doing anything wrong, but what will others think?" Even if you aren't doing anything wrong, use good judgment, because people will remember what they see. Try to step out of your shoes and consider how certain situations will look to others.

Allow Your Actions to Encourage

When you encourage, people see you as someone who truly cares and who wants to see others succeed. Being an encourager gives you an opportunity to help others, while at the same time helping yourself. When people see that you encourage, they will begin to encourage as well, and you become a role model.

A friend of mine was visiting someone in the hospital. When she paid her toll to exit the parking lot, the attendant gave her change and said, "Be encouraged." My friend took these words and remembers them daily. This is the only time she ever saw that attendant, but the words will be with her forever. She left the parking lot with a better outlook on life and a wonderful perception of the attendant.

It's that easy for each of us to be encouragers every day to everyone with whom we come in contact!

When you are working with others, try to give credit to as many people as possible. Don't forget those who do the little things, because they are the people who enable you to concentrate on the big ones. For instance, at every dine-in restaurant, someone is responsible for rolling the silverware. Even though this sounds like a simple job, it is one of the most critical. If a customer receives silverware that is not clean, they will more than likely have a negative perception of the entire restaurant and will not return. Make sure that everyone – from the lowest to the highest positions – knows how important their job is to the success of the business. Don't take the basics for granted.

Walt Disney once said, "You can dream, create, design and build the most wonderful place in the world, but it requires people to make the dream a reality."

Simply Said...

Perception is reality.

- First, maintain composure. Remaining composed is often one of the most effective ways to combat negative situations.
- Second, surround yourself with positive people. As Euripedes said, "Every man is like the company he keeps."
- Third, know that people are always watching. It doesn't matter where you are, what you are doing or what you are wearing, people are always watching you. This is your opportunity to be a role model.
- Fourth, allow your actions to encourage. Being an encourager gives you the opportunity to help others, while at the same time helping yourself.

Coach John Wooden once said, "Be more concerned with your character than with your reputation. Your character is what you really are while your reputation is merely what others think you are." Remember that people's opinions are based on their perceptions.

Wise Words From Others...

We begin to see, therefore, the importance of selecting our environment with the greatest of care, because environment is the mental feeding ground out of which the food that goes into our minds is extracted.

– Napoleon Hill

Success means "showing" what to do rather than "telling" what to do. It means going out in front, going first, and alone if necessary.

– Herbert Kelleher, Chairman of the Board
President & CEO, Southwest Airlines

More than half of it is about morale. If the workers can see me, it helps them personalize this company. And in the end, good morale means good productivity. See and be seen. Get out of your office, walk around, make yourself visible and accessible.

– J.W. "Bill" Marriott Jr.
Chairman & CEO, Marriott International

Be self-assured, or at least act as if you are.

– Dr. Virginia Noelke, Professor, Angelo State University

What people say behind your back is your standing in the community.

— Ed Howe, American Journalist

Conscience is the inner voice that warns us that someone may be looking.

— H.L. Mencken, American Editor

6

All You Have Is Your Name

When we are born, we are given a name – a name that sticks with us from our first breath to our last.

We become associated with and known by this name, and it's how we're identified from here on out. Obviously, there are times when we wish we could have a different name, but all and all, we're stuck with the one we have. Therefore, we should make a conscious and continuous effort to develop a good name along with a good reputation to follow it.

We've all heard the cliché, "Actions speak louder than words." Even though it's challenging, I try to live by this statement. My actions speak for my name. For every action there is a reaction, and your name is always involved in that reaction. We have all had times when we've done something that we weren't proud of. We know how hard it is to keep our slate perfectly clean. But, in my opinion, it's much harder to restore your good name once you've scarred it. This is why we must recognize the importance of treating our name with respect and pride.

I discovered this concept at a fairly early age. When I was in the seventh grade, I had an unfortunate event happen – I had my second date with a girl. Though the event itself wasn't unfortunate, the outcome proved to be. First of all, I was a nervous wreck. I wasn't sure exactly what to do since this was only the second time for me to go out with someone.

My date and I went to the movie at the local theater on a Saturday night. I was so busy trying to figure out if I should put my arm around her or hold her hand or even try to kiss her that I didn't watch much of the movie. The one thought that kept running through my head was that all of my friends made fun of me because I hadn't had my first kiss yet.

Finally I got up from my seat and went to the restroom. I stood in front of the mirror and tried to pump myself up for the attempt at my first kiss. I will never forget how much I was sweating or how many butterflies I had in my stomach. When I thought I was ready, I returned to my seat.

The movie was about half over and I knew if I was going to strike, I had to do it soon. All of a sudden I thought, "Well, here goes nothing." I leaned over and delivered my first kiss. I don't know if it was what I expected, but at least I had finally kissed a girl. I couldn't wait to go back to school and let my friends know so they would quit teasing me.

Everything went downhill from there. The next Monday, when all of the students were standing out in the playground area waiting for first period to begin, I had the bad news delivered to me – she wanted to break up. The first girl I'd ever kissed wanted to break up with me after dating for only one week. She did not give any reason for this drastic action, and that just wasn't good enough for me. It took me the entire day to find out the reason behind the crushing news, but I found out. She told all of her friends that the reason she wanted to break up was because I bit her lip when I kissed her.

For a seventh grader, this was total embarrassment. I was not only rejected by a girl I liked, I was ruined. What little reputation I had gained was shot. Everyone at school seemed to know about Paul's first kissing experience, and they made sure I knew they knew.

Although it took about a month, I was able to get over this horrible experience and gained a valuable lesson through it. I knew in my heart that I did not bite this girl's lip, but it was a struggle every day trying to convince everyone else. I just remember hearing my name associated with something that I certainly did not want to "write home to mom about."

This was when I realized that all I really had was my name, and that how people perceived my actions – whether true or false – reflected on me and my name. I caught on to this then, and it stays with me daily.

My mother has always told me, "You make the bed you sleep in." It took me a long time to understand what she meant by this, but now I know that when I choose a certain action, I am also choosing to accept the responsibility that comes with it. Others will always push you and encourage you to do what they want you to do. But remember, they are not the ones who have to live with the results of your actions. All of my buddies told me I had to have my first kiss, but they were also the ones who made fun of me after I did. They didn't care if I bit the girl's lip or not; they just knew that I was the laughing stock of the school. You have to recognize the fact that no one will take care of your name better than you.

Strive For Honesty

Honesty plays a key role in building your character. There is no bigger word than honesty in my mind, and there is no bigger task than learning how to live an honest life. There are many people who try day-in and day-out to live with honesty and integrity. One of the reasons this is so challenging is that it is human nature to try to get ahead in life, and it's often easier and quicker to get ahead by being dishonest.

For example, think about the stress you felt during your semester exams in school. Generally, you had one solid week of exams testing you over everything you were supposed to have mastered that semester. This was not only in one class, but usually five or six. Ideally, you would have kept up throughout the semester so that you would be somewhat prepared for the test and would not have to burn the midnight oil studying.

If you were unprepared the night before the test, you essentially had two options. The first was stay up all night and cram as much information as possible into your head so that you might be able to get a few correct answers. The second option was go to bed unprepared and cheat on the test. This is a familiar option for many, and this is where some get their first taste of how to get ahead through dishonest means. They continue down this path and end up cheating their way through life. Because they do not take the necessary time to prepare, they feel trapped and then they cheat. Now, what is really gained by cheating? Is it the best solution? You can bet that it is not.

When you cheat in school, you don't learn the material that you are paying someone to teach you. In essence, you are throwing money away. You are being dishonest with yourself and the people around you. You are taking the chance of getting caught and possibly removed permanently from the institution. When you cheat in life, you don't learn the lessons that you are here for, and you are taking the chance of having your name and reputation destroyed.

Recently, I learned an important lesson about dishonesty at a sporting event. I am a total football fanatic when it comes to the Pittsburgh Steelers and had the opportunity to attend one of their games against the Tennessee Oilers. I went with my parents, a friend and his young son who had never attended a professional sporting event. Since he had never had such an experience, we made a point of allowing him to meet as many players as possible. And since I also enjoy collecting autographs, I tried to get all the photos and autographs I could in the few minutes we had with the players.

While we were meeting the team, I had the marvelous fortune of meeting the Steelers' head coach, Bill Cowher. I asked him if he would take a moment to sign a photo that I wanted to give to my older brother for Christmas, and Coach Cowher graciously agreed.

After receiving the signed photo, I asked a young gentleman at the front desk of the elegant hotel if he would please hold it for me while I attempted to obtain other autographs from various players. When I returned to get the photo, it was gone. I was totally shocked and disappointed.

Even though this was an unfortunate experience, I did learn a lesson. It taught me how one person's dishonesty can greatly affect a person they've never even met.

Honesty affects how others see you, and being dishonest will ruin a good name. Aside from discrediting a reputation, it will probably also weigh heavily on your conscience. Remember that you live with the decisions you make.

It's Never Too Late To Turn Over A New Leaf

At some point, we've all been caught with our hand in the cookie jar. We've been caught doing things that wouldn't make our families or ourselves proud. I can remember back to childhood when I would get in trouble for not doing what I was told. My mother would say, "Paul, you better go to bed and turn over a new leaf by morning." I must say that for many years, I did not have any idea what she was talking about. What did turning over a new leaf have to do with disobeying my parents and getting in trouble for it? One day it finally hit me. My mother was offering her forgiveness and giving me a chance to start over. I have been a true believer in turning over a new leaf ever since.

It's easy to say to yourself, "Well, it's too late for me to start over. My name and reputation are shot, and I can't fix what I have destroyed." In my opinion, this is a big excuse and basically a lazy attitude. It is never too late to begin rebuilding anything in life. You first have to tell yourself you are going to rebuild. The process begins by developing the right attitude.

Do you remember when you were a child and got in trouble with your mother or father? Did they ever ask, "Do you need an attitude adjustment?" Essentially, this meant that you had about 30 seconds to change your attitude or you would get that adjustment. Knowing this probably helped you gain a new perspective on the situation. If you didn't change your attitude on your own, a situation that you previously thought was bad was about to get much worse.

It's unfortunate that as adults, we no longer have someone to remind us every time we need to adjust our attitudes. It's generally something that we have to do on our own.

In today's world, the right attitude is a must. It is easy to have a good attitude when everything is going according to how you have planned; the problem arises when things aren't going so well. The phrase "Attitude is everything" is one of the most commonly used "motivational" expressions. Everyone claims that they try to have a good attitude, but for most people, that only lasts until something doesn't go their way. When your plans are thrown off kilter is when you get upset and frustrated, and attitude is the last thing on your mind.

It's interesting to note that the word attitude is derived from an Italian word that means aptitude. I had never thought about it, but it really makes perfect sense. Aptitude is defined as an "inclination, tendency or talent." Often having the right and proper attitude requires much more than a mindset. Sometimes it takes talent. Like other talents, you have to practice having a good attitude every day or you will forget how. When you practice the skill, it becomes easier to have and keep a good attitude – even during the difficult times.

It is completely up to you what type of attitude you want to have each day of your life. When things are not going your way, a good attitude will help pull you through, while a bad one will only discourage you – the choice is yours. Leading by your actions and not so much by your words will help you make a major difference to those who are watching you handle yourself through challenging events.

Your name is all you have, and you must represent it well. Develop the proper attitude to help make changes to yourself when needed. It really is never too late, but you are the only one who has the ability to turn over that new leaf. Sissy Jones, owner of Sissy's Log Cabin, a highly successful jewelry retailer, said, "My opportunity alarm goes off each morning at 5:30 a.m." That's a wonderful way to look at each new day – as an opportunity to begin anew.

Simply Said...

All you have is your name.

- First, strive for honesty. There is no bigger word than honesty in my mind and there is no bigger task than learning how to live an honest life.
- Second, remember it's never too late to turn over a new leaf. It is never too late to begin rebuilding anything in life. You first have to tell yourself you are going to rebuild, and then you have to develop the right attitude to do it.

Your name is all you have, and you must represent it well. Don't be afraid to stand up for your principles and values, as they are a foundation for your name.

Wise Words From Others...

No one can be you but you; no one can be you for you; no one can be you better than you... So, you might as well just be the best you that you can be.

> – Tomonica La-Shai Johnson, Student
> Southern Arkansas University

Be willing to sacrifice time. Work hard but never forget about integrity and honesty. Your word is your bond.

> – John C. Correnti, President & CEO, Nucor Steel

Three lessons of life that I have learned are: First, preparation is more than half of execution. Second, pride is not incompatible with humility. And finally, nothing erodes a base of support more than questions about a person's integrity. Without trust, there can be no sustainable support, particularly when the going gets tough.

> – Robert E. Allen, Chairman & CEO, AT&T

An essential ingredient in gaining the respect and confidence of your associates, board members, suppliers, investing public, and community members is integrity.

> – Michael Goldstein, CEO, Toys "R" Us, Inc.

The ability to deal with all people in a fair and equitable manner and approach issues with an open mind and a caring attitude will lead to success. Truly listen to people and remember there is no substitute for honesty and integrity.

> – Dr. John Smith, Vice President
> University of Central Arkansas

One must never compromise their integrity. Every decision must be based on facts, not hearsay or emotion. A successful person will assess the situation, assemble the facts, analyze all known options and make a decision. A successful person must earn the trust of his or her peers by routinely practicing the principles of hard work, being decisive, as well as having integrity.

> – Norm Mitry, Senior Vice President & CFO
> The Medical Center

I am motivated by the fact that every day I am given the chance to try again!

> – Ollie Wagner, Chaplain
> University of North Carolina, Chapel Hill

Sooner or later, everyone sits down to a banquet of consequences.

> – Robert Louis Stevenson

Honesty is the first chapter of the book of wisdom.

– Thomas Jefferson

The successful man will profit from his mistakes and try again in a different way.

– Dale Carnegie

7

Everyone Has A Story – Ask And Learn

Have you ever stopped for a minute to think about what you have in common with those around you?

Do you come from the same type of background? Do you share the same interests? Do you have similar jobs? We all vary just a bit in our own ways, however there is one thing that everyone in the world has in common – we all have a story of where we've been, where we are and where we are going. Since this is the case, you and I are presented with an incredible opportunity daily – the opportunity to learn!

An essential element in gaining knowledge from those around you is learning to ask questions. Never be afraid to stand up and ask a question. How else do we learn? I meet many people from different vocations every day. I never hesitate to ask how they balance work and family, how they raised their kids or what kinds of things they like to do in their free time. I get all kinds of responses, and this helps me not only to understand others, but to understand myself and how I want to live my life. By simply asking them questions about their lives and their jobs, I am able to gain valuable insight that benefits me.

No Question Is A Stupid Question

You have heard it before, but hear it again! There are no stupid questions.

Growing up, I thought asking questions meant that I was stupid. I thought asking a question would draw all the attention to me, and people would laugh and make fun of me because I did not already know the correct answer. I started asking questions anyway and the exact opposite happened! While I was in college, I realized that asking questions did draw attention to me, but in a positive way, not a negative one. It drew attention to my willingness to learn and not settle for just one answer or concept.

All of a sudden, my professors knew I was in their class to learn and to explore as much as possible. Generally, if you have a question, there is someone else in the room with that same question. Thus, in a sense, you are standing out and being a leader by asking. I also recognized the fact that if I were asking questions, I was rarely called upon. I never really enjoyed being called upon out of the blue, but if I were asking questions and giving my input, it demonstrated to my professors that I was paying attention, and they would call on others.

This is relevant for the business world as well. If you give your input and keep up with what's going on, you generally won't be caught off guard, and you will be that much more effective. Your supervisor will see that you are eager to learn and want to stay on top of your game.

The first thing I did when I started my first job was to go and speak with current employees within the firm. I asked them if they would take a minute to tell me their life stories. I have always been amazed to hear how people not only survive, but thrive, in this complex world. By asking this question, I've heard more than just words; I've grasped concepts that affect me daily.

Many don't ask questions because they don't want to be a bother, but for most people, there is no better compliment than knowing that someone else truly cares and wants to know about them. When a person asks you where you have gained the strength to be a visionary, role model or inspiration, it increases your sense of self-worth.

Give people the opportunity to share with you where they have been and where they plan to go. Some of the stories will amaze you and inspire you, while others will teach you some of the most valuable lessons of life.

In general, people want to tell you their story. All you have to do is ask. When I started writing this book, I knew that I couldn't write a single word about success unless I knew what made people successful. I sat down and brainstormed on how I could gain this information and decided that I would come up with a list of people I thought were successful. I went to the library and located a list of the top companies in America. I then researched the President or CEO and found a mailing address. After I compiled this list, I proceeded to mail hundreds of questionnaires asking about success and the importance of motivation.

And that was just the first mailing. After I had conquered that goal, I sent out a second mailing to successful local people.

Then, I did another mailing. This time to people I knew who I felt had achieved a high degree of success in their fields. Then I stopped, and it hit me that I had just sent out hundreds of letters to people across the country asking them to take time out of their day to respond. What chance did I have to get the attention of some of America's most talented and successful people?

Many couldn't believe that I actually expected people to respond to my questions. They thought it was a waste of my time and money. And, of course, I didn't receive a response from everybody. But I didn't focus on this – the most important thing is that many people did respond! And that was what I focused on.

For several weeks after the last mailing went out, I received numerous responses every day. Most everyone who responded took the questionnaire seriously and put much thought into it. Even if I had decided at that point not to write a book, it's amazing to think of all the lessons I got from such successful people. What I learned from the responses alone would have made my efforts 100% worthwhile.

Successful people usually want to help you succeed. They have already achieved their success and generally don't mind sharing their secrets. Do not be afraid to talk to them and ask what steps they took to achieve their success. The worst that can happen is that they choose not to talk to you. And what have you lost? Absolutely nothing. You are simply one person closer to the one who will talk to you. If you want to learn, you have to ask questions and know that you can't ask too many.

When you ask a person a question, the attention is shifted from you to them. They feel as though they have a sudden purpose and obligation to lead you down the right road. Don't ever think that a question is stupid. Stupidity is found in not asking questions.

Find A Mentor

There is no better way to learn than from a mentor. Find a person, from the past or present, whose purpose in life intrigues you. Watch them closely and mimic each and every step you can from them.

Allow their character qualities to influence your life. If you believe in your mentor's passion toward his or her visions and can learn from it, then having a mentor is a total benefit to you. It is also critical to have someone who will shoot straight with you at all times.

For example, my biggest mentor is my father. I live my life much like he does because I believe in his mission in life. I always know that he is going to be honest with me when I need an honest opinion. He is a man who wants to do his part to make the world a better place and help where he can. Since these are qualities I admire, he is someone I strive to emulate.

Starting out, you might have many mentors in life. As you begin to narrow your focus on what you think your purpose is, you will narrow your mentors as well. You can find these people in many places, and often you will find them when you aren't even looking. For instance, through his books, speeches and other materials, John F. Kennedy has become another mentor of mine.

Remember that mentors are often people who just pass through your life. Several of my past teachers and professors taught me valuable lessons, not just in the subjects they were educated in and paid to teach, but lessons about life. Although those people are not constant in my life any more, I still carry those lessons with me.

If you let yourself become a student of life, the world becomes your mentor. You can gain lessons from every single person around you, if only you will allow yourself. Thinking that you know more than others and that there is nothing that they can teach you only shuts a door that could possibly take you to new worlds.

I know a man who is all business, yet you can go into his office when he is at his busiest and he will stop what he is doing and give you his total attention. I only wish that I could be like that. I once went in and asked how he is able to change focus so quickly without resenting the fact that he is being interrupted. His answer was simple. He said that he learns something from everyone with whom he comes in contact – whether that person has a question, a problem or just wants to talk, he gains knowledge not only about them, but about people in general.

Be observant and open-minded, and you will be amazed at the things you will learn.

Realize the Importance of Listening

In this chapter, I have stressed the importance of asking all the questions you can, while you can. Asking questions is the easy part. The hardest part is listening to the answers you receive and then applying the truths you have heard. Like I've said, people want you to ask them questions, but there is a catch – they only want to take their time to answer your questions if they believe that you are genuinely interested. If you want to show that your curiosity is real, it is imperative that you be a careful listener.

I've asked questions just for the sake of asking and not for the sake of learning. I can assure you that I get much more out of the answers when I ask because I want to understand and comprehend. Asking questions just to ask is a waste of everyone's time, including yours.

When you go into the classroom or the office, do your best to listen to those around you. I'll admit that sometimes I tell people I am listening, when in all honesty, I might not be. I'm sure you can relate. Sometimes it is hard to pay attention when you are thinking about the 50 other things that you need to be doing.

Over the past couple of years, I have been in a professional environment of fast-paced frenzy. I get up in the morning and begin running a hundred before ever hitting the door to the office. Once I am at the office, I ask individuals questions, but at times find myself not sticking around for the answer. I get in too much of a hurry and leave my co-worker's office without all the facts. I even find myself at times finishing others' sentences so the conversation can move along.

Now, asking questions and not sticking around for the answer, as well as finishing others' sentences, is not only rude, it's a waste of time. If you ask a question, then you must be prepared for the answer – short or long. When you find yourself finishing a sentence for a person, consider that you aren't showing them much respect. You are taking away their thoughts, ideas and opinions. We don't like it when others do this to us, so we must try not to do it to others. If you ask someone a question, let him or her answer it.

You must develop the ability to listen. Don't think about your response, don't predict what the other person is going to say and don't interrupt them with your comments. Just listen. By doing this, you will develop respect for the thoughts and words of others. And they will probably return this respect to you.

Simply Said...

Everyone has a story. Ask and learn.

- First, remember no question is a stupid question. Stupidity is found in not asking questions.

- Second, find a mentor. There is no better way to learn than from a mentor. Find someone whose purpose in life intrigues you and learn all you can from him or her.

- Third, realize the importance of listening. When talking with someone, don't think about your response, don't predict what the other person is going to say and don't interrupt him or her. Just listen.

I can assure you that if you ask as many questions as you can of as many people as you can and honestly listen to their answers, you will learn more than any book could ever teach you.

Wise Words From Others...

Anyone who stops learning is old, whether at twenty or eighty. Anyone who keeps learning stays young. The greatest thing in life is to keep your mind young.

– Henry Ford

Who is a wise man? He who learns of all men.

> – The Talmud, a compendium of
> Jewish law, lore and commentary

The experience gathered from books, though often valuable, is but the nature of learning: whereas the experience gained from actual life is the nature of wisdom.

> – Samuel Smiles

I advise all young people to read biographies. Read everything on the subject, interview those who are successful in it, think of ways to improve what has been done in the past, observe everything around you, always keep your eye on solutions, not problems and make up your mind to advise yourself.

> – Dottie Walters, Walters Speaking Service

Listen at least as much as you talk.

> – Dr. Virginia Noelke, Angelo State University

A young person today needs to practice one of the "Star Trek" themes: Learn all that is learnable.

> – Norm Mitry, Senior Vice President & CFO
> The Medical Center

Successful people almost always have education and training, a passion for accomplishing their goals and a plan for achieving it. Education is a critically important foundation for anyone who wants to be successful in today's business environment. It does not matter which discipline you choose, but to be successful you should have the best education and training you can obtain.

– William Cavanaugh III, President & CEO
Carolina Power & Light Company

Life is my college.

– Louisa May Alcott

Knowledge is power.

– Francis Bacon

When you stop learning, stop listening, stop looking and asking questions, always new questions, then it is time to die.

– Lillian Smith, American author

8

Live Your Life
As An Underdog

Have you ever watched the favored team at a sporting event pound the less favored team into the ground or a bout between two boxers when the favored fighter shows no mercy and throws continued body blows until his competitor is knocked clean to the mat?

Most of the time, it's a safe bet to pull for the favorite in sporting events or even in life, but what about those not favored or less fortunate? Who pulls for them?

I have always been amazed by the underdog. We meet under-dogs each day at the office, in school or on the streets – individuals who are not expected to achieve victory because of the odds they must overcome.

I had the opportunity to speak to a group of college students at an engagement in Little Rock, Arkansas. The meeting room was full of three hundred bright students looking to gain valuable tools that would help them get ahead of other students entering the working class. I spoke to this group about the importance of finding a purpose in life that would not only shape their own lives, but also help shape others in a positive way.

After I completed my message, a young man approached me and asked if I would be willing to meet the person who has helped him find his purpose in life. I agreed and, ten minutes later, the young man tapped on my shoulder and introduced me to his friend. Here was a man in his early thirties, well-groomed and well-dressed.

The two of us proceeded with a conversation about the things that motivate him and why he thought life had been good to him. He told me that after a long period of time away from school, he had decided to go back and finish his degree. He attended class part-time and also worked as a student aide.

It might not sound like he was doing anything too spectacular with his life, but in his case, he was. This individual was in an automobile accident at the age of seventeen and was left para-lyzed – unable to do the things so many of us take for granted.

My first thoughts were that he had been cheated out of so many opportunities. He could not run or walk, throw a baseball or catch a football. He spent the majority of his time in a wheel-chair. As I knelt on one knee, he told me the story of how his life was changed through the accident and how he had no complaints. He had been a paraplegic for the past fifteen years and casually said that he was happy with the cards life had dealt him.

After our conversation, the young man who introduced us asked me what I thought. I simply shook my head and said that he could move mountains, let alone minds and imaginations. It was very clear to me how a person like this can and does help others find their purpose in this complex world.

After reflecting on this experience, I respected his willingness to fight the odds of being an underdog and to keep a good attitude. Here was an individual who could sit at home daily and count his losses, but instead he was facing all the barriers, jumping the hurdles life put in his way and moving forward.

As we all know, there are many people just like him. People who have had terrible things happen to them and yet have fought the odds to succeed. But what about the people who have been blessed and fortunate enough not to have a life-changing tragedy happen to them? Are we living our lives day to day and just finding a way to survive or are we going against the odds and making the most of life?

Dreaming The Impossible – Not Just The Possible

I have always been guilty of assuming things will happen the way I anticipate them, both in my personal and my professional life. After endless lessons in life, I have realized that it is more powerful to assume the impossible rather than the possible.

Have you ever been in a situation when you thought you knew what was about to happen? You knew for sure that he or she would call you to ask you out on a date. You were certain you were going to win the award you had been nominated for by your sales team. You were a shoe-in for a promotion that your company was planning to pass down. We've all been in these same situations, and we all know that things don't always happen like we plan. Since this is the case, I have adjusted my train of thought and worked on not assuming so much in life.

When you assume something good is about to happen, it might very well. And if it does, then that's fantastic. But what happens if the good fortune is not sent your way? As we all know, it is a major let-down and disappointment. I enjoy pulling for those who are not as fortunate as the rest.

You can walk into any homeless shelter, nursing home, battered women's shelter or substance abuse center and see the hurt, disappointment and grief in the eyes of the less fortunate. There are many reasons and circumstances that have led these individuals through the doors of such places, but now what do they do? Who will take the time to attempt the impossible? Who will reach out and help pull these people off the mat? I have always assumed that someone else will take on the task of helping those who have not had all the aces dealt to them.

When everyone is assuming that someone else is taking care of the problem, nothing happens. We have to be willing to do the things that no one else wants to do.

Anything is possible. What you achieve is totally up to you. I like to focus on things that others see as impossible, because if I achieve them, I have achieved satisfaction in my own mind. I've done something that no one else thought I could do. This is the underdog in me.

I have been very fortunate in my life and have been totally blessed and privileged. Because of this, it's important that I spend some time in the trenches and try to make impossible things happen. I am not doing my fellow man any good if I do not use the blessings I have been given to help those around me. It doesn't matter how big or how small your contribution is, all that matters is that you are doing something.

Since I have been given many things that I can and should share with others, I believe it is important to give to charity, through both financial support and the contribution of my time. Although many people don't think giving to certain char- itable organizations is worthy of their time or money, do not allow this to distract or discourage you. As long as you believe that you are making the impossible possible, then you are living as an underdog and making a difference.

There Is No One Else Exactly Like You

The fact that there is no other person on this planet exactly like me is the one thought that motivates me daily. It is so fulfilling for me to know that I have control of my destiny and that I do not have to compete with anyone around me. I don't know about you, but I can become quite distracted with people and things in my surroundings. What everybody else is doing and how well they are doing it can and will place automatic pressure on you if you allow it. I try to concentrate on the flip side.

When other people get awards and recognition for their achievements, it's easy to be envious, but understand that these people deserve the awards and achievements they receive. I just have to remember that I am me and that is all I can be. I cannot achieve all things alone, and I try to look at the accomplishments of others not as competition, but as a team member working for the same cause. Will Rogers once said, "We can't all be heroes because somebody has to sit on the curb and clap as they go by." I try to be proud of others' achievements, knowing that I will be rewarded in those or other avenues on another day.

Whether you are truly disappointed or truly satisfied is completely up to you. You are the captain of your ship and the pilot of your aircraft on this journey we call life. You and you alone have the power and the ability to achieve the unimaginable. Don't worry about what others will think, just be the very best you can be and do the very best you can do.

This quote from Dr. Robert Schuller sums it up very well.

"People are unreasonable, illogical, and self-centered. Love them anyway. If you do good, people will accuse you of selfish ulterior motives. Do good anyway. If you are successful, you will win false friends and true enemies. Succeed anyway. Honesty and frankness make you vulnerable. Be honest and frank anyway. The good you do today will be forgotten tomorrow. Do good anyway. The biggest people with the biggest ideas can be shot down by the smallest people with the smallest minds. Think big anyway. People favor underdogs but always follow top dogs. Fight for some underdogs anyway. What you spend years building may be destroyed overnight. Build anyway. Give the world the best you've got and you'll get kicked in the teeth. Give the world the best you've got anyway."

Simply Be Friendly

I strive daily to be as friendly as possible to those with whom I come in contact. People always ask why I bother being friendly to people I don't know. I do it because it matters – to me and to those around me. When I speak at seminars for college students, I try to drive a major concept home to the group I am addressing, *Say hello to as many people as you can.*

This concept sounds pretty basic, but in college, I was amazed at how many people leave their residence halls, go to class, then to the cafeteria and back to their residence halls without ever having a word said to them – and without ever saying a word.

Noticing this, I took on a new mission. When I walked from class to class, I did my best to say hello to as many students as I could. After doing this for a few weeks, the same people who before had never acknowledged my presence would look at me and say "hello" back to me. It wasn't too long before they were talking to me before I had a chance to talk to them. In my own way, I felt like this was making a difference.

When you say a simple hello to someone, they have an automatic sense of belonging. You took the time to notice them. You know how it feels when someone notices you out of the crowd – it feels phenomenal. Being friendly doesn't cost a dime and is one of the quickest ways to set yourself apart from the rest. Yes, there are many friendly people around, but think about how many unfriendly people you come in contact with each day. These types of people are out there, too. Which type of person do you want to be?

This habit of speaking to everyone I see followed me to my professional career. You should see people's faces light up when I say, "Hello, I hope you are having a nice day!" It is so rewarding to make someone smile just because I took a mere second to speak to them.

Of course, you will always have your critics, especially when you are a happy and upbeat person who is saying hello to those around you. I have been called fake and insincere more times than I can count, but I do not let this stop me, because I know that people tear others down to build themselves up. You get knocked down verbally both to your face and behind your back. This is done because many do not have self-confidence in their own lives.

The common thought process is that if I knock you down a few notches, I will build myself up a few. This is simply not true. When a person is talking down about another, they are only hurting themselves. My grandmother once said, "If someone wants to get down in the mud and fight, don't give them the satisfaction of jumping in. When it is all said and done, they will come out muddy and you will still be clean!"

Of course I have my critics, but in my mind, I am achieving rewards on the inside if I can make someone smile. Everyone's entitled to their opinion, but I always recall one thing my brother said to me – you must be doing something right if they are taking the time to stop and talk about you. There will always be negative people out there, but as Finnish composer Jean Sibelius reminds us, "Pay no attention to what the critics say. A statue has never been erected in honor of a critic."

Respect Others

When was the last time you held the door open for a person or said "yes, ma'am" or "no, sir?" Have you ever offered to roll a grocery cart out of a store for an elderly person? We are all guilty of being disrespectful at times. We've talked back to our parents when we should have kept our mouths shut. We've all spouted off to our professors and supervisors when it would have been best just to listen. There is no question that we have all done things we wish we hadn't.

Respect is not the common quality that it once was in our society. People cut in front of others in line, we all use intimidating tones, and we're often selfish. When I got out of college, I was hired to be a salesperson. In this position, I had the opportunity to meet many who respected me and the product that I was trying to sell. However, there always were and always will be those who are not just indifferent about the fact that I was trying to sell them something – they were downright hateful. I know that when I walked into their place of business, I was a salesperson, but the key word here is person. I will always show respect to those around me in turn for the opportunity to earn respect back from them.

It is only fair to give a person the opportunity to make a good first impression. Being respectful is allowing that person to place his or her best foot forward. I will never forget making one of my first sales calls in a well-known resort town in Arkansas. I walked in with a suit on, the publication I was selling in my right hand and a smile on my face. Before I could get my name out, the person behind the desk asked directly, "Are you a salesperson?" I replied, "Yes, sir, I am." He immediately and hatefully responded, "Well, you can leave now. I do not like salespeople and, by the way, I do not like where you parked your vehicle." I was totally shocked and ready to let this guy have it. But instead I honored his request, turned around and headed straight to the door. When I got to the door, I turned and told the man to have a very nice day.

As I drove away, I became upset and couldn't figure out why anyone would be so rude and disrespectful. After I cooled down, I reflected on the entire incident and understood that his attitude had nothing to do with me. He was not disrespecting me, he was disrespecting the salesperson in me. When I realized this, I was thankful that I had walked in the door and shown the man some respect and, even though I was upset, I had left the same way. I can only hope that showing him some respect helped him see the person instead of the salesperson and just maybe he did have a better day.

Learn To Handle Rejection

I will be the first person to admit that I, like most, do not handle rejection well. Being turned down, told no or kicked out of an establishment goes straight for the ego. You know what it feels like to study for days for a big exam and come up short when the professor hands back your paper. And there is nothing like going into a sales meeting with a client and presenting what you feel is an awesome plan or strategy, only to have the client look at you like you just fell off the turnip truck.

Rejection will test anyone's self-esteem.

I have always told people that there are a few steps that we all must attempt to follow when trying to accomplish a sale, a perfect test score or any other task that could end with rejection.

First, be comfortable with yourself. You have to be able to look yourself in the mirror and say you can accomplish the task at hand. You have to be committed. If not, the odds aren't with you. I'm sure you have heard people say that you have to love yourself before you can love anyone else. That is so true, and I also believe that you have to be comfortable with yourself before you can accomplish any task.

Second, believe in the task that you are trying to accomplish. I had the opportunity to interview Bonnie Blair, the Olympic gold medalist speed skater. She said:

> "You have to believe in your product. If you are going to do something or sell something, you have to love it and believe in it. If you do not believe in what you are trying to accomplish, sell or teach, you might as well hang it up."

I am truly convinced of this. You cannot approach anything half-speed and expect to be successful. If you are going to dance, then dance. Don't sit around waiting to be asked.

Third, and probably the most important part of attempting a goal and facing rejection, is to know that you are going to win some and lose some. When I make calls to potential clients, I know that they will either say "yes" or "no." But I also know that, even if they say "no," I will always have someone else to call on.

One of my colleagues told me one thing to always keep in mind when I was selling. He said, "Paul, every 'no' you receive is one call closer to a 'yes'!" At first, I didn't understand what he meant, but after being turned down by the best of them, I learned never to quit knocking on doors and asking for new business.

It is a safe bet to say that rejection will always be a part of life. Those who handle it well will have the opportunity to move forward. There was once an advertisement for United Technologies Corporation that well demonstrated that rejection will happen, but you have to keep going. It read:

An irate banker demanded that Alexander Graham Bell remove "that toy" from his office. That toy was the telephone. A Hollywood producer scrawled a rejection note on a manuscript that became *Gone With the Wind*. Henry Ford's largest original investor sold all his stock in 1906. Roebuck sold out to Sears for $25,000 in 1895. Today, Sears may sell $25,000 of goods in 16 seconds.

You and I will be turned down in our personal and professional lives more times than we can count. But as this ad illustrates, it is the person who keeps going who will ultimately succeed.

Be A Class Act

Have you ever been around a person who can enter a room and gain the automatic attention of everyone? I am mesmerized by such people. When I have the opportunity to be around these types of individuals, one word comes to mind – class! If you have class, you have something that will set you apart from the crowd.

It does not take much effort to be a class act. Many think of people with class as those who are well-off financially and who have been successful in their fields. I disagree. Having a few manners, respecting others at all costs and walking the walk instead of just talking the talk are super starts down the road of class.

I recently visited a nursing home and watched a man interact with his wife. She was in a wheelchair, and he was pushing her down the hall. He was dressed in a suit and looked very nice. This man had class written all over him from first glance. He had no other reason to wear a suit except for the fact that he was coming to see his wife and wanted to look nice for the most important person in his life.

We often take the people who are important to us for granted when in all actuality they are the ones who we should show the most respect to, be the most honest with and take the most care of. This is class.

Always Treat People As Though They Have Had A Bad Day

I really like the concept of treating people as though they've had a bad day. When you stop to think about it, if you treat people like this on the front end, you will always be treating them with the utmost respect and kindness. There are times your temper will flare and you will lose sight of this, but having patience and composure with people will only help you be the type of positive person you want to be.

It doesn't matter if you are speaking to someone on the telephone or in person, take the time to put yourself in their shoes and ask yourself how you would like to be treated. Your actions and words will always relay a sense of kindness and understanding if you apply this simple concept.

Simply Said...

Live your life as an underdog.

- First, dream the impossible, not just the possible. Believe that you can make the impossible happen and work toward that goal.

- Second, remember that there is no one else exactly like you. Since there is no one else like you, take comfort in the fact that you do not have to compete with anyone and can do anything you choose to do.

- Third, simply be friendly. Being friendly doesn't cost a dime and is one of the quickest ways to set yourself apart from the rest.

- Fourth, respect others. Show respect to those around you and in return you will earn the opportunity to gain respect back from them.

- Fifth, learn to handle rejection. Rejection will always be a part of life. Those who handle it well will be able to move forward.

- Sixth, be a class act. Have a few manners, respect others at all costs and walk the walk instead of just talking the talk.

- Seventh, always treat people as though they've had a bad day. Do this and you will always be giving others the utmost respect.

If you live your life as an underdog, simply trying to be the best you can be, you will quit worrying about what others think and quit trying to keep up with what others are doing. Expect the best, but do not assume that everything will happen the way you planned it.

Wise Words From Others...

You can't hold a man down without staying down with him.

– Booker T. Washington

How we think shows through in how we act. Attitudes are mirrors of the mind. They reflect thinking.

– David Joseph Schwartz

No one can hurt you, unless you accept the hurt in your own mind.... The problem is not the other people; it is your reaction.

– Vernon Howard

In helping others, we shall help ourselves, for whatever good we give out completes the circle and comes back to us.

– Flora Edwards

Getters don't get – givers get.

– Eugene Benge

All doors open to courtesy.

– Thomas Fuller

What sunshine is to flowers, smiles are to humanity. They are but trifles, to be sure; but, scattered along life's pathway, the good they do is inconceivable.

– Joseph Addison

No man has ever risen to the real stature of spiritual manhood until he has found that it is finer to serve somebody else than to serve himself.

– Woodrow Wilson

Get in the habit of kindness. When kindness is built into your life, it will not seem remarkable nor will it be extra effort. It will just be the way you are. Everyone in your life will behave toward you based on that idea of who you are. Don't compare yourself to anyone else. Don't have secret "kindness meter" which is always judging yourself. If someone else does a great act of kindness, don't compete with it, join it, learn from it, copy it gratefully, extend it.

– Hanoch McCarty, Ed.D., Author

Success is derived from a passion for the possible, a willingness to go the extra mile, gladly and with no thought of personal gain, a sense of the limitless capacity of all human beings, a love for people, and the passion to serve them.

– D. Trinidad Hunt, International Speaker, Author

Having the respect of people is a prerequisite for the successful leader. Employees respect those they love. In order to be admired, a successful leader must first show love.

Herbert Kelleher, Chairman of the Board,
President & CEO, Southwest Airlines

Put yourself in the other person's shoes. Look at a problem from both sides. "Real life is not black or white, right or left, top or bottom. Most solutions lie in the middle and are gray in color."

– John C. Correnti, President & CEO, Nucor Steel

Simply be nice to others.

– Mike Harrison, Owner, Norfork Trout Dock

Work hard to advance other people and in the process you advance yourself. Be open to possibilities and stay somewhat flexible. Hard work and persistence is critical.

– Dr. John V. Griffith, President
Presbyterian College

9

You Only Live Once

Though we rarely stop to think about it, we know we only get one shot at the challenge of life. This sole thought will either motivate your heart and soul to be the best you can or it will intimidate you enough to make you not even try. I must say that I have mixed emotions when I think about only living once. I know in my heart that there are so many things that I want to accomplish, but I wonder if I will have enough time to do them. Only God knows the answer.

I'm good at making mountains out of molehills. I seem to find ways to make the small things into bigger ones and spend the majority of my time thinking and worrying about them. Since this is the case, you could say that I waste much of my time worrying about how the chips will fall instead of just letting them.

I comprehended how absurd this was one evening while popping a bag of microwave popcorn. I set the timer on the microwave for four minutes. As I stood there waiting for the popcorn to pop, the timer went off and suddenly it hit me. Four minutes of my life had passed that quickly. I know four minutes doesn't seem like much, but it is still four minutes that I will never have back. This is when I realized that I shouldn't spend so much precious time concerned about all of the little things.

Ralph Waldo Emerson once said, "We are always getting ready to live, but never living." We need to spend as many minutes as we can doing the things that are worthwhile in our lives. We only have so many minutes on this earth. So my question to you is, what are you doing with yours?

Love What You Do

During the interview with Bonnie Blair, I asked what motivates her each day when she hits the ice. She simply said, "I love what I do." She made it very clear to me that you have to love what you do if you are going to be successful doing it. She commented, "There were days when things went wrong with my skating, and there were days that my feet and the skates felt like they were one. It is easy to love what you do on the good days, but you have to reach deep down to find love for what you do on the not-so-good days."

Since there are only twenty-four hours in a day, we must be very selective about what we sink our teeth into. Knowing that we only live once should motivate us to make the best of what we do each and every day. It all starts with love toward the things you do. If you love what you are doing, and you are doing your very best, you are making a difference, because people around you will notice your enthusiasm and feed off of it.

If you aren't doing something that you love, consider changing what you are doing. It's scary to take a leap of faith on the hopes that you will truly be happy doing something else. The risk is worth the outcome if you are able to get up every morning and be happy and enthusiastic about what you are doing.

Let Enthusiasm Work For You

When everything is going your way, it is easy to get up in the morning, smile and have the best attitude in the world. But what do you do when things aren't going your way? What happens when life throws you a curve ball and you can't hit it? This is when enthusiasm steps in! People love to be around those who build others up. There are so many people who bring others down; one person with an enthusiastic attitude can brighten an entire room.

I am one of the biggest believers in the power of enthusiasm. I look forward to getting up in the mornings and getting the day started. Doing this gives me an immediate advantage over the many people who never get excited about what they are doing. Look around the next time you are walking down the street. You will pass people who have dazed looks on their faces, their chins facing down toward the ground and their shoulders slouching. These people need a dose of enthusiasm.

A person with enthusiasm and a love for life has so much to offer. After I graduated from college, I had the wonderful opportunity to interview with one of the largest advertising agencies in the South. One of the very first questions I was asked was, "Paul, what can you bring to the table to help this company grow in the right direction?" I knew that I was not immediately going to be bringing in loads of money for the agency; I did not have the experience in marketing and advertising. I had some basic fundamentals from college, but zero experience in the "real world." What I did know was that I could bring the element of enthusiasm.

After thinking about the question for a minute, I responded, "Well, I might not be one of your big-time salespeople and my bottom line might not reflect the best results, but I will be a battery pack of enthusiasm that your twenty-year veterans can feed off. Those salespeople have the experience, but some might be lacking a little pick-me-up. That would be my beginning role." I got the job – and the opportunity to live up to my promise.

Having a love for life and living it with enthusiasm gives you the opportunity to be in a class by yourself. It gives you the chance to help change lives and it is something that you have complete control over. Once you have recognized this power, you will have a source you can use over and over again.

Follow Your Vision

Having a vision is amazing, but useless if you don't follow it to the sweet or bitter end. Many people have sight; few have true vision. A vision is much like a dream. To live the life you want to live, you first have to dream it up in your own mind and believe in the power of passion to see it through. I took a minute to really focus on this after seeing a quote from Franklin D. Roosevelt. He once said, "To accomplish great things we must not only act, but also dream, not only plan, but also believe." I think we would all be a little better off if we not only read such a quote, but acted upon it.

I read an article about George Clooney, the actor who has become well-known through his roles on television's "ER" and several movies. The article clearly depicted that Mr. Clooney has had his share of disappointments and losses throughout his life. But through it all, he stated that one of the key things he has learned is, "The only failure is not to try." I don't think it could be said any better. Like President Roosevelt said, you have to act upon your dreams and believe that you can obtain the possible – along with the impossible. You cannot know the boundaries of the possible until you exceed them.

A famous quote by Ben Mays well states this idea of chasing a dream.

> "It must be borne that the tragedy in life does not lie in not reaching your goal, but tragedy lies in having no goal to reach. It isn't a calamity to die with dreams unfulfilled but it is a calamity not to dream. It is not a disaster to not be able to capture your ideal, but it is a disaster to have no ideal to capture. It is not a disgrace not to reach the stars, but it is a disgrace to have no stars to reach for. Not failure, but low aim is sin."

There are no limits to anyone's vision or dreams as long as you attempt to pursue them. I have always lived with the dream of communicating to people through my speaking and writing. In my mind, if I do not chase this dream with a passion and a love, then I am cheating myself. If you are blessed with a vision and a passionate drive to reach it, you have no choice but to do it.

A prime example to better explain vision is the relationship between light and darkness. When you close your eyes, naturally you do not see anything. There is complete darkness. Everything becomes motionless. When you have no vision, it is like being shut out of the world. In this analogy, light represents vision. Light enables you to see what is around you and to clearly see which direction you want to go.

Once you have your vision and direction, don't spend the majority of your time looking back. In a speech given by Arkansas Governor Mike Huckabee, he said, "I've often thought as I sit in the front seat of a car that the windshield is much larger proportionally than is the rearview mirror. And maybe there is a lesson for life there. The rearview mirror is important for an occasional glance to see what's behind and to keep up with the traffic that may be gaining, but it would be a disastrous thing indeed to spend most of one's time focusing on where we have been rather than focusing on where we are going. And that's why the windshield is far bigger and gives a much better view than does the rearview mirror."

You must know where you are going and what steps you are going to take to get there. Once you know, you just have to do it.

A good example of following your vision is illustrated by the actor Brad Pitt. At the end of his senior year at the University of Missouri at Columbia, Brad was one paper short of graduating, yet he left because he knew in his heart it was time to move on. "In my head, I was done with college," Pitt said. "I was on to the next thing, and that was acting." He had a vision and followed it with a passion.

Some people are born with their vision, while others have to search. In order to clarify what your vision is, try writing all your dreams and aspirations down on a sheet of paper. Once you have a list, review it and update it regularly. Make a mental picture of exactly what your vision is, focus on that and share it with others. It is good to have encouragement during the times when you want to give up – from someone who can give you that extra push when you need it.

George Bernard Shaw said it well when he coined the quote, "Some men see things as they are and ask why? I dream things that never were and ask why not?" Don't be afraid to follow your vision with passion.

How Will You Be Remembered?

"How do you want to be remembered?" is a question that I often ask myself and others around me. It is somewhat intriguing to listen to all the answers you hear.

"I want to be remembered as a person who made a difference to those around me." "I want to be remembered as the top sales-person for our company." "I want to be remembered as a person who served others well day-in and day-out." "I want to be remembered as the best baseball player ever to swing the bat."

You hear a variety of responses to this question. More important than the answers others give is your own answer. Ask yourself how you want to be remembered and then strive for that.

Read the book, *Don't Sweat the Small Stuff, And It Is All Small Stuff*, by Dr. Richard Carlson. Here you will find the chapter: "Remind Yourself When You Die, Your In Basket Won't Be Empty."

How true this is!

One of the questions that the author brings out is, "Do you think that you are going to be laying on your death bed wishing you had spent more time at the office?" I am as guilty as anyone when it comes to working those late hours, but I don't want those hours to control my life.

I understand how much concentration it takes to be effective in an occupation, but I also realize that often the people in my life need that time even more. Dr. Carlson made a great point: your in basket will always have room for more. Give your very best to your occupation but do your best not to forget those wonderful people around you.

Nobody knows when his or her time is up!

You can turn on the news and hear about a recent murder, read the paper about a train crash or listen to a radio report of a tragic tornado on any given day.

Since this is reality, let's make the best of it while we can and do things that will last in the memories and hearts of many long after we have left this world.

You can make an everlasting impression on many through giving your time, talents and God-given gifts. People remember those who gave to them in their own ways. Focus on your everyday goals and dreams, but in so doing, ask yourself if you are honestly leaving an impression that will last through today as well as tomorrow.

Time Is Precious

There have been many days in my life that I thought were worthless from the start. Days when nothing seemed to be going right. On days such as these, I let my mind wander back in time to a saying that my father taught me when I was worried that I was not going to make the varsity football team in the eighth grade. He sat on the corner of my bed and said, "Son, I want you to remember one thing. It is never so bad that it couldn't be worse!"

Now, I know that many people would think that worrying about making the varsity football team in the eighth grade isn't worth the worry, but for me it was knowing in my mind that I could accomplish a goal. More than that though, I learned a valuable lesson through the ordeal thanks to my father.

From that point forward, "It's never so bad that it couldn't be worse" has been a life motto.

It stays in my mind when I get stressed over the big things, as well as the small. I have realized that you can't allow yourself to take your days for granted, no matter how difficult they may be. Since we know this, we need to strive to take care of ourselves and nurture each day we're given. My mother once gave me a quote along these same lines. The quote goes something like this:

"Yesterday is history.

Tomorrow is a mystery.

Today is God's gift – that's

why it's called the present.

Make the most of it."

Knowing that things could always be a little worse motivates me to do the very best with what I have. Look around the next time you go out. Most likely, you will see someone in the crowd who is a little worse off than you. Often, others' misfortunes will remind us to be thankful for what we have been given and will motivate us to improve ourselves while helping others to improve themselves. Open a door for a handicapped person or help a blind person across a street.

Through these types of actions, you will not only be helping someone in a kind way, you will also appreciate what is in my opinion one of the primary aspects of your life – your health. As well as teaching me that things could always be worse, my father taught me the importance of health. He has always said, "If you have your health, you have the ability to do anything."

I can't imagine not being able to get out of bed in the morning on my own or not being able to go jogging down the street at night. Many are not able to do either. They have been stripped of the opportunity to even try. Take advantage of each day that you can do these things, while at the same time doing your best to take care of yourself physically and mentally. Get the proper rest needed to be productive and be determined to stay in good physical health. You and I have been given only one body and the ability to use it. Let's do our best to take care of it, while helping ourselves and others, because, "it's never so bad that it couldn't be worse."

Simply Said...

You only live once.

- First, love what you do. If you aren't doing something you love, consider changing what you are doing. The risk is worth the outcome if you are able to get up in the morning and be happy and enthusiastic about what you are doing.
- Second, let enthusiasm work for you. A person with enthusiasm and a love for life has so much to offer.
- Third, be passionate. Vision is useless if you don't follow it with your whole heart.

- Fourth, how will you be remembered? Ask yourself how you want to be remembered and then strive for that. Make the best use of your time so that you will be remembered in the hearts and memories of others after you are gone.
- Fifth, know that time is precious. Remember that it's never so bad that it couldn't be worse and never take a single day for granted. You never know when it will be your last.

We only get one shot at the challenge of life. Let this thought motivate you to be the very best you can be while you are here.

Wise Words From Others...

I'd rather be a failure in something that I love than a success in something that I don't.

– George Burns

Where there is no vision, the people perish.

– Bible, Proverbs 29:18

There is little sense of wasted time when you have arrived at a life situation in which you enjoy the great majority of the hours you spend doing something that you have chosen to do. You can then live in the present instead of always longing for the future.

– Dr. George Lankford, Professor, Lyon College

Make your vocation your avocation.

– Art Linkletter, Entertainer

You are the master of your own future and are responsible for your own happiness. Find a career that you will become passionate about and develop your plan for success. Strive for excellence; anyone can be mediocre.

William Cavanaugh III, President & CEO
Carolina Power & Light Company

The most important thing in achieving success is truly enjoying your work.

Dr. Win Thompson, President
University of Central Arkansas

No matter what you do in life, swing for the fences.

– Ron Robinson, Of Counsel
Cranford Johnson Robinson Woods

The Final Lesson Is Up To You

Piecing a puzzle together is a challenge. But the puzzle makers give us a head start by putting a picture of how the finished product should look on the front of the box. In life, we aren't given a picture of how we are supposed to turn out. We have been given an even greater gift – the ability to choose what we want our finished product to be, along with the power to achieve it.

The lessons shared in this book illustrate how you first have to define the person you want to be. Then you must become that person. Live your life with integrity. Follow your heart. Acquire habits that you believe to be good ones. And respect the people around you.

You will travel many paths in the search for success, money, the perfect spouse, the best job and so forth. For each accomplishment, there will be failure, and for each choice, a new set of circumstances. Don't become discouraged, for when your search leads to your own happiness, success will find you and you will have achieved more than many ever will.

When you find happiness, your purpose for living will become clear, your direction in life will become more evident and you will be able to live your life the way you want through your actions as well as your words and spirit. Then you will lead others through the lessons that impacted you.

The lessons in this book consist of the thoughts, ideas and concepts that help me maintain clarity of purpose and keep me on track during my own search for happiness.

Simply said, these lessons work for me, but the final lesson is up to you.

You have to decide for yourself what lessons you will apply in your life. I challenge you now to take a moment and decide what you want your final picture to be and what steps you are going to take in the pursuit of your purpose.

You Can't Finish Unless You Begin

What are you passionate about in your life?

_____

_____

_____

What areas do you need to become more disciplined in to help you reach your goals?

_____

_____

_____

What are five lessons (ideas, thoughts, concepts) that you live by daily?

_____

_____

_____

What areas of your life do you want to improve?

_____

_____

_____

List five individuals whom you believe you could learn from and rely on to be a mentor.

_____

_____

_____

What qualities would you want to learn from them?

_____

_____

_____

How can you encourage those around you?

_____

_____

_____

Who could you place a simple phone call to and make their day?

_____

_____

_____

What are your top five dreams that make your heart open and your imagination soar?

_____

_____

_____

Lessons I've Learned From Others

It's better to deserve honors and not have them than to have them and not deserve them.

– Mark Twain

There's no right way to do something wrong.

– Unknown

Live by the do-right rule. If you do right, you don't have anything to worry about.

– Shelby Woods, Chairman of the Board
Cranford Johnson Robinson Woods

For everything you have missed, you have gained something else; and for everything you gain, you lose something else.

– Ralph Waldo Emerson

Concentrate all your thoughts upon the work at hand. The sun's rays do not burn until brought to a focus.

– Alexander Graham Bell

Nothing can be done except little by little.

– Charles Baudelaire

The starting point of all achievement is desire. Keep this constantly in mind. Weak desires bring weak results, just as a small amount of fire makes a small amount of heat.

– Napoleon Hill

Every man is an impossibility until he is born.

– Ralph Waldo Emerson

Always be planning something.

– John A. Schindler

It's so hard when I have to, and so easy when I want to.

– Sondra Anice Barnes

The difference between a successful person and others is not a lack of strength, not a lack of knowledge, but rather a lack of will.

– Vince Lombardi

Failure to prepare is preparing to fail.

– John Wooden

If a man is called to be a streetsweeper, he should sweep streets even as Michelangelo painted, or Beethoven composed music, or Shakespeare wrote poetry. He should sweep streets so well that all the hosts of heaven and earth will pause to say, here lived a great streetsweeper who did his job well.

– Martin Luther King, Jr.

Success takes integrity, dependability, hard work, a good memory, a sense of humor, paying attention to detail without losing sight of the "big picture," caring about other people, and doing things for others while being careful not to get used up by their needs. Don't shy away from or explain away praise, but keep in mind the old saying, "There's no limit to what you can accomplish if you don't care who gets the credit for it."

– Dr. David Stricklin, Professor, Lyon College

You must have ability, desire and work ethic. Select a company that is the best in your field of interest and be prepared to take any job offered to you, no matter how demeaning it might seem at the time. Let them know that you are in for the long-term not the short-term. Be prepared to give 500% of yourself to your job or creation. Make yourself indispensable. You will definitely be noticed. I think this applies to any field and is what an employer wants today. If you are truly interested in a career and not just a job, you will make a place for yourself.

– Patti Upton, Aromatique

Work hard at the ground level. The young person who sets their goals and strives with diligence to reach them can succeed.

– Mitchell Collins, D.D.S. M.D.

Always know who your champion is.

Wayne Woods, Executive Vice President
Cranford Johnson Robinson Woods

Remember, nothing works without determination. Success is not for the ambivalent. It's for those who know what they want and go after it, no matter how difficult the path.

– Alex Trotman, Chairman of the Board
Ford Motor Company

Who needs motivation when you love what you do and the people you work with?

– Robert Martin, Executive Vice President of Marketing
Applebee's International, Inc.

The job of a leader is to recognize the potential of his followers.

– Frank Cox, President and CEO
Cranford Johnson Robinson Woods

One must have self-knowledge and a deep certainty that one's work is well-suited to his or her temperament. True success is the realization that constant learning brings constant triumph. Be happy and secure so you may help others succeed.

– Dr. Bart Lewis, Professor, Lyon College

Follow your heart, work hard and love what you do and who you serve. These three ingredients will bring you to great success, not as the world measures it, but as your own heart measures it. Happiness and joy will always follow the one who loves and follows his or her heart.

– D. Trinidad Hunt, International Speaker, Author

To be successful in life one has to be persistent, patient and have the ability to be able to learn from his or her mistakes. Don't focus too tightly.

– Jonathan Bates, M.D., CEO
Arkansas Children's Hospital

What motivates me every day is a relentless pursuit of excellence for our company. I do not believe that you achieve excellence by chance, and that is why I stress planning so passionately.

– William Cavanaugh III, President & CEO
Carolina Power & Light Company

Know how to lead. Leadership is more than "authority"; it's courage, vision, ethics, and a grounding in reality as well. Think about leadership. Read about it. Study it in the leaders you respect. It's important.

– Alex Trotman, Chairman of the Board
Ford Motor Company

Follow your heart and you can't fail.

– Brenda Scisson, Executive Vice President
Cranford Johnson Robinson Woods

I believe each of us has a talent to put to work to find ourselves and in the finding, help others. Some ignore their talents, some let friends talk them out of their gifts as not being "practical." Sadly, too many forgo their inherent genetic ability in the mindless pursuit of money.

– Ray Bradbury, Novelist

When you are part of a senior management team there are no excuses, no one else to blame, no scape goats. "You" have the power to facilitate the organization into action. That is very motivating.

– Norm Mitry, Senior Vice President & CFO
The Medical Center

The trick to being successful is figuring out how to win by the rules rather than losing because you weren't willing to try a different approach. People who play to win get things done. People who play to make a point or become a martyr generally don't accomplish anything but that.

– Richard W. Davies, Executive Director
Arkansas Department of Parks & Tourism

Learn to read, write, and listen effectively. You must read and comprehend to learn and stay current in your field. You must be able to communicate well in order to sell your ideas and you must be able and willing to listen well if you are to work successfully with others.

– Robert Young III, President & CEO
Arkansas Best Freight

Success is getting what you want, yet wanting what you get. Many people feel they will be successful when their net worth is at a certain level or a material goal is met. Yet, once they have achieved these goals, it turns out not to be what they expected nor really wanted. Such a person is not "successful." They have merely achieved a goal.

– Henry Nichols, President
Central and Southern Companies, Inc.

Success is reaching toward one's potential (infinite) and contains a major element of service.

— Ben Burton, Speaker, Author

Conflicts will arise, but your attitude will play a major role in the outcome.

— Dr. John Smith, Vice President
University of Central Arkansas

The central motivation is to get better. There is no such thing as stasis in human behavior. You either improve or decline. I hope every day that what I write will be better than what I have written before, and that as a teacher I will find better ways to impart knowledge.

— Ernest Dumas, Professor
University of Central Arkansas

The ability to communicate your message clearly whether verbally or in writing is an essential ingredient for success as a manager.

— Michael Goldstein, CEO
Toys "R" Us, Inc.

Know your stuff. Study hard at your chosen profession. Master its skills. Today's working world is an intensely competitive place and knowledge is the basic price of admission. Think and compete globally. Markets, capital, technology, information and products increasingly ignore national borders. You need to learn about other cultures – how they think, how they communicate, how they do business. A second language is good; a third better.

– Alex Trotman, Chairman of the Board
Ford Motor Company

Success is to find oneself turning out well as a person first and then as a part of society. The standard of success is not in achievements, awards or prosperity, although these are fine. Success is knowing that you have given your best in the task of living and contributing to your family and community.

– Rex Horne, Pastor
Immanuel Baptist Church

Never miss an opportunity to educate yourself in your chosen field.

– Judge Charles Yeargan

Find a job interesting to you, that you can learn from, and that can keep you busy. The worst thing in the world is to be bored.

– James Simpson III, Senior Vice President
Stephen's, Inc.

Success is a state of mind, not a destination. It builds on what you have accomplished or accomplish. Never be satisfied until you have given your very best. Great leaders are often not the ones who had the highest grades in school or had the highest SAT scores; instead they are those who work hard, do their best, keep discovering, developing new talents, often pushing themselves to failure in some endeavor and very importantly they persevere. They will not quit, they stay the course until they accomplish the goal. They persevere.

– R.W. Allen, President & CEO
Delta Airlines

It all begins with you.

– Hank Phelps, Student Life
University of Central Arkansas

Be flexible but durable.

– Skip Rutherford, Executive Vice President
Cranford Johnson Robinson Woods

He who permits himself to tell a lie once, finds it much easier to do it a second time.

– Thomas Jefferson

It's better to be defeated on principle than to win on lies.

– Arthur Caldwell

Paul Vitale is the founder of Vital Communications, Inc. He is a native of Russellville, Arkansas and received his degree in Mass Communications and Journalism from the University of Central Arkansas. Paul travels around the globe speaking to universities, school districts, corporations and associations about the importance of a positive attitude, strong work ethic and concepts vital to personal and professional success. His expertise, energy and ability to encourage people to exceed their potential have been described by his audiences as extraordinary.

Paul has authored several books, developed a handful of curriculums and published the first in a series of CD recordings. In his spare time, Paul enjoys volunteering with Big Brothers/Big Sisters, Children's Hospital and the Cystic Fibrosis Foundation. Paul is a graduate of Leadership Greater Little Rock and was named one of the "40 under 40" by *Arkansas Business*.

Heather Ericson, a Little Rock native, graduated from Lyon College in 1996. She works as a Case Manager for Centers for Youth and Families, and in her spare time enjoys writing, helping construct presentations for Vital Communications and volunteering with Big Brothers/Big Sisters and Arkansas Children's Hospital.

For Additional Copies

If interested in additional copies of *Are You Puzzled by the Puzzle of Life?*, they may be ordered directly from Vital Communications, Inc., at 501-868-8195 or online at www.paulvitale.com.

Also by Paul Vitale

Pass It On - Quotations for all Generations
Are You Puzzled by the Puzzle of Life? Teacher's Guide
Dazzle Them With Customer Service Teacher's Guide
Professional Presentation Coaching Guide
Live Life Like You Mean It Audio CD
A Hero Within Complete Curriculum Kit

For additional information on these products as well as Paul Vitale's seminars and presentations, please contact Vital Communications, Inc., at www.paulvitale.com.

Thank you for your interest!